INDIVIDUAL PRACTICE SETS

WfT

West's Federal Taxation

1998 - 1999 Editions

William H. Hoffman, Jr.
J.D., Ph.D., C.P.A.
University of Houston and State University

Eugene Willis
Ph.D., C.P.A.
University of Illinois at Urbana

James E. Smith
Ph.D., C.P.A.
College of William and Mary

William A. Raabe
Ph.D., C.P.A.
Samford University

David M. Maloney
Ph.D., C.P.A.
University of Virginia

Prepared by
Mark Nixon
Ph.D.
Bentley College

West / South-Western College Publishing
an International Thomson Publishing company I(T)P®

Cincinnati • Albany • Boston • Detroit • Johannesburg • London • Madrid • Melbourne • Mexico City
New York • Pacific Grove • San Francisco • Scottsdale • Singapore • Tokyo • Toronto

Accounting Team Director: Richard K. Lindgren
Acquisitions Editor: Alex von Rosenberg
Developmental Editor: Esther Craig
Production Editor: Rebecca Glaab
Marketing Manager: Maureen L. Riopelle
Manufacturing Coordinator: Gordon Woodside

ISBN: 0-538-88900-4

1 2 3 4 5 6 7 WST 4 3 2 1 0 9 8

Printed in the United States of America

ITP®
International Thomson Publishing
West/South-Western College Publishing is an ITP Company.
The ITP trademark is used under license.

TABLE OF CONTENTS

PREFACE

These practice sets are designed to be used with the West's Federal Taxation Series. However the material covered in the practice sets is common to most introductory textbooks on federal taxation. Since the practice sets are comprehensive and require a substantial text coverage, they should be assigned near the end of the term.

The practice set includes most of the common forms used by taxpayers. The forms are perforated so they can be removed from the booklet to make completing the forms easier.

The student should begin the practice set with the forms that lead to the calculation of Adjusted Gross Income (Schedules B,C,D,E,SE). Then the student should proceed to Schedule A and related forms. Selected tax rate schedules, depreciation schedules and other information is also provided.

I hope these practice sets will be as useful as possible. I will appreciate all comments and suggestions.

Mark R. Nixon

INDIVIDUAL PRACTICE SET #1

REED AND LINDA PETERSON

FEDERAL TAX RETURN

1. Reed (age 63, social security #568-72-6070) and Linda (age 62, social security 903-51-3955) Peterson presently live at 675 Harrison Road, Waltham, MA 02254. Reed is an Assistant Vice President at Makemore Electronics and Linda owns and manages a local franchise for H&R Block. Although Linda is a tax professional, the Peterson's always have another tax professional prepare their personal return. You have been engaged to prepare their 1997 tax return. The Peterson's choose not to contribute to the presidential election campaign fund.

The Petersons have two children. Rick (age 18, social security # 568-72-5050) is the manager of a large car wash in Waltham. His annual salary is $34,000 per year. He lives at home and puts his entire paycheck into an investment account. Crystal, age 24, social security number 234-21-7360, is a full-time student at Bentley College. Her parents pay for her tuition, all of her living expenses and provide her with a car. She works for her mother during the summer and holidays full-time. She earned $9,800 in 1997.

2. Linda owns an H&R Block franchise (employer number 87-2458914, business code #7633) at 4545 Beacon Road, Waltham, MA 02455. She uses the cash basis of accounting, except for cost of goods sold. Her income and expenses for the year are:

Collections from tax returns prepared	$181,000
Collections from sale of business software	48,000
Lease payments on business location	18,000
Speeding ticket while delivering tax returns	120
Utilities	4,200
State income taxes for Peterson's 1996 joint return	5,000
Telephone	6,400
Advertising	4,800
Customer entertainment	1,500
Franchise fee to H&R Block	14,000
Employee wages	54,000
Payroll taxes	8,000
Health insurance premiums for employees	5,000
Office supplies	4,000
Software inventory purchased for resale	33,000
Insurance	2,400

Charitable contributions to Bentley College........................	2,800
Repairs on office equipment (includes computers)................	2,200
Legal fees..	4,000

	Beginning Inv.	Ending Inv.
Software inventory	$19,000	$9,000

Prior to 1997, Linda's business purchased the following equipment. The adjusted basis at the time of purchase (AFTER any applicable reduction for Sec. 179 expense):

Computers (4), May-1994, $3000 each	(total $12,000)
Office equipment (misc.), June-1992	$16,000
Office equipment (misc.), Sept-1995	$12,000
Office equipment (misc.), July-1989	$15,000
Purchased in 1997:	
Copy machine, August 8, 1997	$ 6,500*

On May 1, 1997 Linda sold two of the computers purchased in 1994 for $1,500 each. On May 10, 1997 she traded two of the computers for a sophisticated computer system. She had to pay an additional $19,000* for the network system. Linda has always used the fastest capital recovery methods available.

* Section 179 deduction not yet taken for 1997.

On July 24th, an individual crashed their car into the rear of the office and set off the automatic sprinklers. The landlord repaired the building costing $16,000. However, the water damaged client files. The cost to replace client files was $8,000. Insurance reimbursed Linda $5,500.

During 1996 Linda settled a lawsuit with a former customer by agreeing to pay $9,000. The lawsuit was due to a former employee divulging confidential information to the customer's competitor. She paid 1/3 of the settlement in December 1997. The balance will be paid in 1998. She has errors and omissions insurance, but chose not to file a claim.

3. During February 1993 Linda's Uncle Mike (Kane) borrowed $9,000. He was repaying the loan at $150 per month including 10% interest. The unpaid principal amount at the beginning of the year was $6,700. Uncle Mike made only one payment during this year ($94 principal, $56 interest), but claims he will get caught-up soon. However, Reed and Linda are not sure that they will be repaid.

4. On September 15, 1997 Linda sold 150 shares of common stock she owned in Look Sharp Corporation for $750. Linda had received the stock as a gift from her sister, Gail, on April 15, 1992. Gail had purchased the stock in 1988 for $3,200. When Gail gave the stock to Linda the fair market value was $2,475.

Other securities sold during the year (all common stock):

Property	Date Acquired	Purch. Price	Date Sold	Sales Price
100 Seal Corp.	5/6/96	$6,000	3/1/97	$7,400
200 Light Corp.	3/3/96	3,300	10/25/97	2,700
500 Goodman Corp.	11/11/83	7,700	3/1/97	8,800

5. Linda has equity interest in a partnership and an S Corporation. The respective K-1s are attached.

Electronics Research, Ltd., Linda worked only 110 hours in 1997. However, for 1997, she worked more than any other individual in the company.

Tax-Kwik Software, Inc., Linda does not have any idea how many hours she spent working for the corporation, however, she has been a material participant in the corporation for the last six years.

6. The following were paid out of the Peterson's checkbook:

Dentist bills for Rick	$ 375
Automobile insurance premiums	3,700
Sales tax on new auto purchase (received a $1,000 cash rebate on new auto purchase)	850
Subscription to "Tax Planner" magazine	75
Political contribution to Ed Swift's campaign for Mayor of Waltham	400
Personal interest on Discover credit card	660
Mortgage interest for their personal residence (interest paid to Fleet Mortgage Company)	6,900
Real estate taxes on residences	3,500
Hospital bills in excess of reimbursement	2,500
Medical prescriptions (amount unreimbursed)	245
Tax return preparation fee by Always Right Tax Service (Peterson's personal tax return is always prepared outside of Linda's office). Of the total fee, $625 applies to Linda's business	1,095

Safe deposit box for stock	35
Life insurance premium	7,800
Dues paid to Gold's Gym for exercise class	450
Contribution to St. John church	5,500
Automobile personal property tax	235

7. The Peterson's gave various used clothing to Goodwill Industries (original cost $900, estimated FMV = $450). The Petersons have all receipts from Goodwill and kept a detail list of items donated.

8. Reed used his personal automobile for charitable use in behalf of the Cancer Society, 950 miles. Reed spent 75 hours in volunteer service for the Cancer Society. He figures his time was worth $1,125 to the organization.

9. Reed had 3,400 miles of unreimbursed business travel this year. The total miles driven on his car was 12,000 miles including 5,000 miles for commuting. Reed kept a log supporting his mileage, but does not keep records of actual costs of operating the auto. He purchased his car in 1995. Reed and Linda own three cars. Reed also had $875 of unreimbursed business entertainment expenses.

10. Total medical miles driven during the year, 620.

11. Linda made four estimated tax payments, for 1997, $3,000 each, totaling $12,000 to the Internal Revenue Service.

12. Dividends received from Lucky Corp. $900. Dividend earned on life insurance policy, $85.

13. Interest earned on savings account at College Credit Union, $550. (Amount credited to the savings account on 12/31/97, but not withdrawn until February 1998).
Interest earned on Waltham City tax anticipation revenue bonds, $1,500.
Interest earned on 6 month U.S. Treasury Note (matured 10/97), $750.

14. The State of Massachusetts audited the Petersons for tax year 1995. They found the

Petersons had overstated their tax liability and refunded them $1,200. In 1995, the Petersons reported $5,500 in state income taxes paid on Schedule A.

15. The Peterson's have provided you with all necessary W-2s, K-1s and 1099s.

a Control number | OMB No. 1545-0008

b Employer's identification number 47-6532188	1 Wages, tips, other compensation 67,000	2 Federal income tax withheld 7,200
c Employer's name, address, and ZIP code Makemore Electronics 789 North Avenue Waltham, MA 02254	3 Social security wages 65,400	4 Social security tax withheld 4,054.80
	5 Medicare wages and tips 67,000	6 Medicare tax withheld 971.50
	7 Social security tips	8 Allocated tips
d Employee's social security number 568-72-6070	9 Advance EIC payment	10 Dependent care benefits
e Employee's name, address, and ZIP code Reed Peterson 675 Harrison Road Waltham, MA 02254	11 Nonqualified plans	12 Benefits included in box 1
	13 See Instrs. for box 13	14 Other
	15 Statutory employee ☐ Deceased ☐ Pension plan ☐ Legal rep. ☐ Hshld. emp. ☐ Subtotal ☐ Deferred compensation ☐	

16 State	Employer's state I.D. No.	17 State wages, tips, etc.	18 State income tax	19 Locality name	20 Local wages, tips, etc.	21 Local income tax
MA	34256	67,000	2,400			

Department of the Treasury—Internal Revenue Service

Form **W-2** Wage and Tax Statement **1997**

This information is being furnished to the Internal Revenue Service.

Copy B To Be Filed With Employee's FEDERAL Tax Return

☐ CORRECTED (if checked)

PAYER'S name, street address, city, state, ZIP code, and telephone no.		1a Gross dividends and other distributions on stock (Total of 1b, 1c, 1d, and 1e)	OMB No. 1545-0110	Dividends and Distributions
Lucky Corporation 298 West Avenue Boston, MA 00963		$ 900	1997	
		1b Ordinary dividends $ 900	Form 1099-DIV	
PAYER'S Federal identification number 74-9872345	RECIPIENT'S identification number 903-51-3955	1c Capital gain distributions $	2 Federal income tax withheld $	Copy B For Recipient
RECIPIENT'S name Linda Peterson		1d Nontaxable distributions $	3 Foreign tax paid $	This is important tax information and is being furnished to the Internal Revenue Service. If you are required to file a return, a negligence penalty or other sanction may be imposed on you if this income is taxable and the IRS determines that it has not been reported.
Street address (including apt. no.) 675 Harrison Road		1e Investment expenses $	4 Foreign country or U.S. possession	
City, state, and ZIP code Waltham, MA 02254		Liquidation Distributions		
Account number (optional)		5 Cash $	6 Noncash (Fair market value) $	

Form 1099-DIV (Keep for your records.) Department of the Treasury - Internal Revenue Service

Instructions for Recipient

Box 1a.—Gross dividends include any amounts shown in boxes 1b, 1c, 1d, and 1e. If an amount appears in box 1c or 1d or both, you must file **Form 1040.** If you file **Form 1040A,** report the amount in box 1a. If you file **Schedule 1 (Form 1040A)** or **Schedule B (Form 1040)** to report dividends, report the amount in box 1a. If you file **Form 1040** without **Schedule B,** report the sum of boxes 1b and 1e on the "Dividend income" line of **Form 1040.** Also report the amount in box 1c on Schedule D (Form 1040) or on the "Capital gain or (loss)" line of Form 1040 (write "CGD" on the dotted line).

The amount shown may be a distribution from an employee stock ownership plan (ESOP). Although you should report the ESOP distribution as a dividend on your income tax return, treat it as a plan distribution, not as investment income, for any other purpose.

Box 1b.—Ordinary dividends are fully taxable and are included in box 1a. This may include net short-term capital gains from a mutual fund.

Box 1c.—Capital gain distributions (long-term) are included in box 1a.

Box 1d.—This part of the distribution is nontaxable because it is a return of your cost (or other basis). You must reduce your cost (or other basis) by this amount for figuring gain or loss when you sell your stock. But if you get back all your cost (or other basis), you must report future nontaxable distributions as capital gains, even though this form shows them as nontaxable. This amount is included in box 1a. For more information, see **Pub. 550,** Investment Income and Expenses.

Box 1e.—Any amount shown is your share of the expenses of a nonpublicly offered regulated investment company, generally a nonpublicly offered mutual fund, which is included as a dividend in box 1a. The full amount shown in box 1a must be reported as income on your tax return. If you file Form 1040, you may deduct the expenses shown in box 1e on the "Other expenses" line on **Schedule A (Form 1040)** subject to the 2% limit. Generally, the actual amount you should have received or had credited to you is the amount in box 1a less the amount in box 1e.

Box 2.—Shows backup withholding. For example, persons not furnishing their taxpayer identification number to the payer become subject to backup withholding at a 31% rate on certain payments. See **Form W-9,** Request for Taxpayer Identification Number and Certification, for information on backup withholding. **Include this amount on your income tax return as tax withheld.**

Box 3.—You may choose to claim the amount shown as a deduction or a credit. See **Pub. 514,** Foreign Tax Credit for Individuals.

Nominees.—If your Federal identification number is shown on this form and the form includes amounts belonging to another person, you are considered a nominee recipient. You must file Form 1099-DIV for each of the other owners showing the income allocable to each, and you must furnish a Form 1099-DIV to each. File Form(s) 1099-DIV with **Form 1096,** Annual Summary and Transmittal of U.S. Information Returns, at the Internal Revenue Service Center for your area. On each Form 1099-DIV, list yourself as the "payer" and the other owner as the "recipient." On Form 1096, list yourself as the "filer." A husband or wife is not required to file a nominee return to show amounts owned by the other.

☐ CORRECTED (if checked)

PAYER'S name, street address, city, state, ZIP code, and telephone no.		Payer's RTN (optional)	OMB No. 1545-0112	
College Credit Union 246 Lewis Waltham, MA 09271			**1997** Form **1099-INT**	**Interest Income**
PAYER'S Federal identification number 53-9872345	RECIPIENT'S identification number 568-72-6070	1 Interest income not included in box 3 $ 500		**Copy B** **For Recipient** This is important tax information and is being furnished to the Internal Revenue Service. If you are required to file a return, a negligence penalty or other sanction may be imposed on you if this income is taxable and the IRS determines that it has not been reported.
RECIPIENT'S name Reed Peterson		2 Early withdrawal penalty $	3 Interest on U.S. Savings Bonds and Treas. obligations $	
Street address (including apt. no.) 675 Harrison Road		**4 Federal income tax withheld** $		
City, state, and ZIP code Waltham, MA 02254		5 Foreign tax paid $	6 Foreign country or U.S. possession	
Account number (optional)				

Form **1099-INT** (Keep for your records.) Department of the Treasury - Internal Revenue Service

SCHEDULE K-1 (Form 1065)
Department of the Treasury
Internal Revenue Service

Partner's Share of Income, Credits, Deductions, etc.

► See separate instructions.

For calendar year 1997 or tax year beginning , 1997, and ending , 19

OMB No. 1545-0099

1997

Partner's identifying number ► 903-51-3955

Partnership's identifying number ► 87 : 0010066

Partner's name, address, and ZIP code

Linda Peterson
675 Harrison Road
Waltham, MA 02254

Partnership's name, address, and ZIP code

Electronica Research, Ltd
314 Share Drive
Cambridge, MA 02220

A This partner is a ☒ general partner ☐ limited partner ☐ limited liability company member

B What type of entity is this partner? ► Individual

C Is this partner a ☒ domestic or a ☐ foreign partner?

D Enter partner's percentage of:

	(i) Before change or termination	(ii) End of year
Profit sharing	%	50 %
Loss sharing	%	50 %
Ownership of capital	%	50 %

E IRS Center where partnership filed return: Andover, MA

F Partner's share of liabilities (see instructions):

Nonrecourse	$ -0-
Qualified nonrecourse financing	$ -0-
Other	$ 25,000

G Tax shelter registration number ►

H Check here if this partnership is a publicly traded partnership as defined in section 469(k)(2) ☐

I Check applicable boxes: (1) ☐ Final K-1 (2) ☐ Amended K-1

J **Analysis of partner's capital account:**

(a) Capital account at beginning of year	(b) Capital contributed during year	(c) Partner's share of lines 3, 4, and 7, Form 1065, Schedule M-2	(d) Withdrawals and distributions	(e) Capital account at end of year (combine columns (a) through (d))
23,000	-0-	2,150	(10,000)	11,550

		(a) Distributive share item		(b) Amount	(c) 1040 filers enter the amount in column (b) on:
Income (Loss)	1	Ordinary income (loss) from trade or business activities	1	3,000	See page 6 of Partner's Instructions for Schedule K-1 (Form 1065).
	2	Net income (loss) from rental real estate activities	2		
	3	Net income (loss) from other rental activities	3		
	4	Portfolio income (loss):			
	a	Interest	4a	50	Sch. B, Part I, line 1
	b	Dividends	4b		Sch. B, Part II, line 5
	c	Royalties	4c		Sch. E, Part I, line 4
	d	Net short-term capital gain (loss)	4d	4,500	Sch. D, line 5, col. (f)
	e	Net long-term capital gain (loss):			
		(1) 28% rate gain (loss)	e(1)		Sch. D, line 12, col. (g)
		(2) Total for year	e(2)		Sch. D, line 12, col. (f)
	f	Other portfolio income (loss) *(attach schedule)*	4f		Enter on applicable line of your return.
	5	Guaranteed payments to partner	5		See page 6 of Partner's Instructions for Schedule K-1 (Form 1065).
	6	Net section 1231 gain (loss) (other than due to casualty or theft):			
	a	28% rate gain (loss)	6a		
	b	Total for year	6b		
	7	Other income (loss) *(attach schedule)*	7		Enter on applicable line of your return.
Deductions	8	Charitable contributions (see instructions) *(attach schedule)*	8		Sch. A, line 15 or 16
	9	Section 179 expense deduction	9		See page 7 of Partner's Instructions for Schedule K-1 (Form 1065).
	10	Deductions related to portfolio income *(attach schedule)*	10		
	11	Other deductions *(attach schedule)*	11		
Credits	12a	Low-income housing credit:			
		(1) From section 42(j)(5) partnerships for property placed in service before 1990	a(1)		Form 8586, line 5
		(2) Other than on line 12a(1) for property placed in service before 1990	a(2)		
		(3) From section 42(j)(5) partnerships for property placed in service after 1989	a(3)		
		(4) Other than on line 12a(3) for property placed in service after 1989	a(4)		
	b	Qualified rehabilitation expenditures related to rental real estate activities	12b		See page 8 of Partner's Instructions for Schedule K-1 (Form 1065).
	c	Credits (other than credits shown on lines 12a and 12b) related to rental real estate activities	12c		
	d	Credits related to other rental activities	12d		
	13	Other credits	13		

		(a) Distributive share item		(b) Amount	(c) 1040 filers enter the amount in column (b) on:
Investment Interest	14a	Interest expense on investment debts	14a		Form 4952, line 1
	b	(1) Investment income included on lines 4a, 4b, 4c, and 4f	b(1)		See page 8 of Partner's Instructions for Schedule K-1 (Form 1065).
		(2) Investment expenses included on line 10	b(2)		
Self-employment	15a	Net earnings (loss) from self-employment	15a	3,000	Sch. SE, Section A or B
	b	Gross farming or fishing income	15b		See page 9 of Partner's Instructions for Schedule K-1 (Form 1065).
	c	Gross nonfarm income	15c		
Adjustments and Tax Preference Items	16a	Depreciation adjustment on property placed in service after 1986	16a		See page 9 of Partner's Instructions for Schedule K-1 (Form 1065) and Instructions for Form 6251.
	b	Adjusted gain or loss	16b		
	c	Depletion (other than oil and gas)	16c		
	d	(1) Gross income from oil, gas, and geothermal properties	d(1)		
		(2) Deductions allocable to oil, gas, and geothermal properties	d(2)		
	e	Other adjustments and tax preference items *(attach schedule)*	16e		
Foreign Taxes	17a	Type of income ▶			Form 1116, check boxes
	b	Name of foreign country or possession ▶			Form 1116, Part I
	c	Total gross income from sources outside the United States *(attach schedule)*	17c		
	d	Total applicable deductions and losses *(attach schedule)*	17d		
	e	Total foreign taxes (check one): ▶ ☐ Paid ☐ Accrued	17e		Form 1116, Part II
	f	Reduction in taxes available for credit *(attach schedule)*	17f		Form 1116, Part III
	g	Other foreign tax information *(attach schedule)*	17g		See instructions for Form 1116.
Other	18	Section 59(e)(2) expenditures: **a** Type ▶			See page 9 of Partner's Instructions for Schedule K-1 (Form 1065).
	b	Amount	18b		
	19	Tax-exempt interest income	19		Form 1040, line 8b
	20	Other tax-exempt income	20		See page 9 of Partner's Instructions for Schedule K-1 (Form 1065).
	21	Nondeductible expenses	21		
	22	Distributions of money (cash and marketable securities)	22		
	23	Distributions of property other than money	23		
	24	Recapture of low-income housing credit:			
	a	From section 42(j)(5) partnerships	24a		Form 8611, line 8
	b	Other than on line 24a	24b		

Supplemental Information

25 Supplemental information required to be reported separately to each partner *(attach additional schedules if more space is needed)*:

SCHEDULE K-1 (Form 1120S)

Department of the Treasury Internal Revenue Service

Shareholder's Share of Income, Credits, Deductions, etc.

▶ See separate instructions.

For calendar year 1997 or tax year beginning , 1997, and ending , 19

OMB No. 1545-0130

1997

Shareholder's identifying number ▶ 903-51-3955

Corporation's identifying number ▶ 88 1234000

Shareholder's name, address, and ZIP code

Linda Peterson
675 Harrison Road
Waltham, MA 02254

Corporation's name, address, and ZIP code

Tax-Kwik Software, Inc.
1616 Freedom Way
Cambridge, MA 02220

A Shareholder's percentage of stock ownership for tax year (see instructions for Schedule K-1) . . . . ▶ 15 %
B Internal Revenue Service Center where corporation filed its return ▶ Andover, MA
C Tax shelter registration number (see instructions for Schedule K-1) . . . . ▶ N/A
D Check applicable boxes: **(1)** ☐ Final K-1 **(2)** ☐ Amended K-1

	(a) Pro rata share items		**(b)** Amount	**(c)** Form 1040 filers enter the amount in column (b) on:
Income (Loss)	1 Ordinary income (loss) from trade or business activities	1	(2,000)	See pages 4 and 5 of the Shareholder's Instructions for Schedule K-1 (Form 1120S).
	2 Net income (loss) from rental real estate activities	2		
	3 Net income (loss) from other rental activities	3		
	4 Portfolio income (loss):			
	a Interest	4a		Sch. B, Part I, line 1
	b Dividends	4b		Sch. B, Part II, line 5
	c Royalties	4c	2,000	Sch. E, Part I, line 4
	d Net short-term capital gain (loss)	4d		Sch. D, line 5, col. (f)
	e Net long-term capital gain (loss):			
	(1) 28% rate gain (loss)	e(1)		Sch. D, line 12, col. (g)
	(2) Total for year	e(2)		Sch. D, line 12, col. (f)
	f Other portfolio income (loss) *(attach schedule)*	4f		(Enter on applicable line of your return.)
	5 Net section 1231 gain (loss) (other than due to casualty or theft):			
	a 28% rate gain (loss)	5a		See Shareholder's Instructions for Schedule K-1 (Form 1120S).
	b Total for year	5b		
	6 Other income (loss) *(attach schedule)*	6		(Enter on applicable line of your return.)
Deductions	7 Charitable contributions *(attach schedule)*	7	125	Sch. A, line 15 or 16
	8 Section 179 expense deduction	8		See page 6 of the Shareholder's Instructions for Schedule K-1 (Form 1120S).
	9 Deductions related to portfolio income (loss) *(attach schedule)*	9		
	10 Other deductions *(attach schedule)*	10		
Investment Interest	11a Interest expense on investment debts	11a		Form 4952, line 1
	b (1) Investment income included on lines 4a, 4b, 4c, and 4f above	b(1)		See Shareholder's Instructions for Schedule K-1 (Form 1120S).
	(2) Investment expenses included on line 9 above	b(2)		
Credits	12a Credit for alcohol used as fuel	12a		Form 6478, line 10
	b Low-income housing credit:			
	(1) From section 42(j)(5) partnerships for property placed in service before 1990	b(1)		Form 8586, line 5
	(2) Other than on line 12b(1) for property placed in service before 1990	b(2)		
	(3) From section 42(j)(5) partnerships for property placed in service after 1989	b(3)		
	(4) Other than on line 12b(3) for property placed in service after 1989	b(4)		
	c Qualified rehabilitation expenditures related to rental real estate activities	12c		See pages 6 and 7 of the Shareholder's Instructions for Schedule K-1 (Form 1120S).
	d Credits (other than credits shown on lines 12b and 12c) related to rental real estate activities	12d		
	e Credits related to other rental activities	12e		
	13 Other credits	13		

For Paperwork Reduction Act Notice, see the Instructions for Form 1120S. Cat. No. 11520D **Schedule K-1 (Form 1120S) 1997**

		(a) Pro rata share items		(b) Amount	(c) Form 1040 filers enter the amount in column (b) on:
Adjustments and Tax Preference Items	14a	Depreciation adjustment on property placed in service after 1986	14a		See page 7 of the Shareholder's Instructions for Schedule K-1 (Form 1120S) and Instructions for Form 6251
	b	Adjusted gain or loss	14b		
	c	Depletion (other than oil and gas)	14c		
	d	(1) Gross income from oil, gas, or geothermal properties	d(1)		
		(2) Deductions allocable to oil, gas, or geothermal properties	d(2)		
	e	Other adjustments and tax preference items *(attach schedule)*	14e		
Foreign Taxes	15a	Type of income ▶			Form 1116, Check boxes
	b	Name of foreign country or U.S. possession ▶			
	c	Total gross income from sources outside the United States *(attach schedule)*	15c		Form 1116, Part I
	d	Total applicable deductions and losses *(attach schedule)*	15d		
	e	Total foreign taxes (check one): ▶ ☐ Paid ☐ Accrued	15e		Form 1116, Part II
	f	Reduction in taxes available for credit *(attach schedule)*	15f		Form 1116, Part III
	g	Other foreign tax information *(attach schedule)*	15g		See Instructions for Form 1116
Other	16	Section 59(e)(2) expenditures: **a** Type ▶			See Shareholder's Instructions for Schedule K-1 (Form 1120S).
	b	Amount	16b		
	17	Tax-exempt interest income	17		Form 1040, line 8b
	18	Other tax-exempt income	18		See page 7 of the Shareholder's Instructions for Schedule K-1 (Form 1120S).
	19	Nondeductible expenses	19		
	20	Property distributions (including cash) other than dividend distributions reported to you on Form 1099-DIV	20		
	21	Amount of loan repayments for "Loans From Shareholders"	21		
	22	Recapture of low-income housing credit:			
	a	From section 42(j)(5) partnerships	22a		Form 8611, line 8
	b	Other than on line 22a	22b		

Supplemental Information

23 Supplemental information required to be reported separately to each shareholder *(attach additional schedules if more space is needed)*:

Line #7 - Cash contribution to United Way, 50% limitation.

REQUIREMENTS

Prepare the Peterson's 1997 federal income tax return, with supporting schedules and attachment. Use the following assumptions in preparing the return:

1. Use the whole dollar method for all forms.

2. Use all opportunities to minimize the 1997 federal income tax.

3. Disregard any possible penalties for underpayment of estimated taxes (Form 2210).

4. Do not prepare Form 6251 (Alternative Minimum Tax).

5. Do not prepare a state income tax return.

6. Use the Tax Rate Schedules for the calculation of the tax liability, even though the form may require use of Tax Tables.

7. Not all information in the fact set has an impact on the final tax liability. However, the purpose of this project is to expose you to various aspects of tax law, not simply to get the correct tax liability. Therefore, when a form calls for information of the type provided in the fact set, complete the appropriate parts of the form even though the item may have no final effect on the tax liability. This includes the preparation of any worksheets suggested by the forms or instructions. For example, Form 2106 (unreimbursed employee expenses) should be completed even though the total miscellaneous itemized deductions do not exceed 2% of adjusted gross income.

INDIVDUAL PRACTICE SET #2

SCOTT AND JAN RUCKER

FEDERAL INCOME TAX RETURN

1. Scott (age 53; social security number 568-34-1110) and Jan (age 53; social security number 568-76-6065) Rucker reside at 26 Willis Lane, Waltham, MA 02154. Scott owns and operates a restaurant in Waltham. Jan works for the state of Massachusetts as an ombudsman for the Consumer Protection Agency. They want you to prepare their 1997 federal income tax return. They do not elect to contribute to the Presidential Election Campaign Fund.

2. None of the Rucker's children live at home. They only provide over 50% support for one child, Karen, age 21 (Soc.Sec # 528-73-7123). She is a full-time accounting student at Bentley College, Waltham, MA. Karen earns $12,500 per year as the accountant for her father's restaurant, see #9 below. The Rucker's also provide over half the support for two orphan children living in Peru. Scott's mother, Alice(age 78, Soc .Sec # 568-72-6000), receives her primary support from Scott and Jan. Alice lives in her own home in New Hampshire and receives $5,300 in social security per year.

3. The State of Massachusetts pays 100% of the premiums for Jan and Scott's medical insurance as a fringe benefit. The value of the premiums for 1997 was $3,300. Jan had $20 per month deducted from her payroll as a contribution to the United Way. For Jan's position, the agency does not provide any expense account. However, Jan felt is was necessary for her to occasionally take individuals involved in controversies to lunch, for which she paid a total of $300 during the year. She often had to go to various locations in Massachusetts to make investigations. None of her travel was over night.

Jan's travel costs:	Meals....................	$600
	Speeding ticket(s).......	175

Jan drove her personal car (1994 Oldsmobile) to all her agency appointments. Her auto had a total of 22,000 miles during the year, including 6,500 miles of agency business and 8,400 miles of commuting (28 miles round trip). Jan did keep a written log of her travel, but did not keep track of actual auto expenses.

4. On May 1st the Ruckers purchased a home in Waltham for $266,000. On May 15th, they moved from Springfield, MA to their current address in Waltham, MA, a

distance of 150 miles. The Rucker's sold their house at 555 Walter Ave., Springfield, MA 02380, on June 15th for $295,000. Real estate commissions were $17,700. They had purchased the home on August 15, 1985 for $165,000. From prior home sales they had deferred recognition of gain on sale of personal residence of $56,000. In order to get a lower interest rate for the Waltham home, at closing they paid 3 points on a $200,000 mortgage loan from Fleet Bank

Jan was promoted to Senior Ombudsman, and now works in Boston, 15 miles from her residence. Her former office in Springfield was 6 miles from her home. Jan's employer, State of Massachusetts, provided a $2,200 moving allowance, *the State did not include the moving allowance in her Form W-2.* Prior to moving the Ruckers took two house hunting trips to Waltham. Their hotel, meals and transportation expenses were $675. For the actual move, the cost of transporting their belongings was $3,300. Jan and Scott each drove their own car from Springfield to Waltham. Their new house was not ready to occupy when they arrived, so they had to stay in a hotel for four days. Total cost for hotel and meals while waiting to move in were $475.

5. The Ruckers had a valuable original oil painting they had purchased in 1985 for $19,000. The painting was purchased as an investment and was part of the Rucker's retirement portfolio. They did not want to include the painting in the moving van. So they put it in Scott's car for the trip to Waltham. While they were stopped for dinner Scott's car was broken into and the painting stolen. The Ruckers filed a police report and an insurance claim. The current fair market value of the painting was $26,000, however the insurance policy had a maximum recovery of $18,000, which was paid.

6. Scott owned and operated a restaurant called "Grilling" in Springfield. Prior to moving Scott investigated two locations for a new restaurant in the Boston area. He selected a location at 154 Trapello Road, Waltham, MA 02154. The IRS business code for restaurants is 3079. His tax I.D. number for the restaurant is 87-1234555. He operates the restaurant on the cash basis of accounting. The Waltham restaurant kept the same name. The cost of investigating each location was $1,900.

7. Prior to moving, Scott closed his restaurant in Springfield. However, he sold several pieces of restaurant equipment on 3/31/97:

Description	Date Purchased	Cost	Basis 12/31/96	Sales Price
Walk-in freezer	3/1/96	$26,000*	$22,286	$19,500
Commercial oven	9/1/95	12,000**	-0-	8,000

* Section 179 election not claim in 1996.
**Expensed in 1995 under Section 179 election.

8. Scott purchased the following piece of restaurant equipment for the new location in Waltham:

Description	Date Purchased	Cost
Walk-in freezer	5/1/97	$33,000

9. Scott's only piece of business equipment he took with him to the Waltham location was a computer system (100% business use). He purchased the computer system on October 31, 1996 for $4,500.

10. The revenue and expenditures, per the "Grilling" checkbook are listed below for 1997 are detailed below, amounts include both locations:

Revenue	$875,000*
Food costs	315,000
Labor costs	230,000
Payroll tax expenses	34,500
Lease expense - building	40,000
Lease expense - equipment and fixtures	25,000
Springfield Health Department	3,000**
Insurance	15,000
Advertising	65,000
Supplies	22,000
Utilities	27,000
Bank charges, including credit card fees from customer charges	13,900
City business licenses	800
State of Massachusetts income taxes for 1996	1,900***
Repairs and maintenance	8,400
Accounting and payroll tax return preparation	12,500****

*This the <u>gross deposits to the bank</u>. See # 11 below for bad checks received during the year.

**Grilling had several heath code violations. Scott paid $3,000 in fines. All violations were fixed before the next inspection.

*** This is the balance of taxes due the State of Massachusetts for Jill and Scott's 1996 income tax return, paid 4/15/97. Ninety percent of the amount is related to income earned by the restaurant.

**** Paid to Karen Rucker, daughter of Scott Rucker.

11. Included in the food purchases above, Scott contributed $400 of food for a church banquet. He contributed the use of restaurant plates and utensils and his time as chef. The value of the use of the supplies and Scott's time was $450. The church provided Scott the proper documentation for a charitable contribution.

12. For 1997, Scott has $850 in bad checks from customers. He has no expectation of ever collecting on the bad checks.

13. Below are various expenditures from the Rucker's personal checking account:

Contributions to United Church of Waltham	$ 5,500
Estimated federal income tax payments (4 payments of $2,500)	10,000
Estimated Massachusetts State income taxes (4 payments of $500, the fourth payment was made on January 15, 1998.)	2,000
Mortgage interest on personal residences (paid to Fleet Bank)	9,700
Property taxes on personal residences	3,900
Principal paid on mortgage loans	1,550
Automobile personal property tax (2 cars, nonbusiness)	437
Automobile insurance premiums (2 cars, nonbusiness)	2,300
Interest paid on automobile loans (2 cars, nonbusiness)	2,700
Dues paid to Gold's Gym for exercise class	450
Medical prescriptions (amount unreimbursed)	255
Hospital and doctor bills (amount reimbursed by insurance company, $5,000)	6,600
Safe deposit box rental	45
Tax return preparation fee, of the total fee 75% applies to Scott's restaurant	800

14. The Ruckers have no capital investment transactions in 1997, but do have a net short-term capital loss carryover from 1996 of $5,500.

15. The Rucker's other income for 1997 is summarized below:

Interest income from certificate of deposit at Springfield State Bank	$ 850
Rebate from the purchase of a new car for Jan	1,500
Interest income from Waltham School District bonds	1,000

Gambling winnings	$ 900
Gambling losses	(1,700)

The Ruckers do not have any foreign bank accounts or interest in foreign trust accounts.

16. Scott is one of several general partners in AutoProfit, a computer software company specializing in restaurant management software. Scott worked 325 hours on partnership affairs, more than anyone else. The K-1 from the partnership is attached.

a Control number	
OMB No. 1545-0008	
b Employer's identification number	04-1327060
c Employer's name, address, and ZIP code	Commonwealth of Massachusetts 120 Cambridge Street Boston, MA 01110
d Employee's social security number	568-76-6065
e Employee's name, address, and ZIP code	Jan Rucker 26 Willis Lane Waltham, MA 02154

1 Wages, tips, other compensation	55,000	2 Federal income tax withheld	4,600
3 Social security wages	55,000	4 Social security tax withheld	3,410
5 Medicare wages and tips	-0-	6 Medicare tax withheld	798
7 Social security tips	-0-	8 Allocated tips	
9 Advance EIC payment		10 Dependent care benefits	
11 Nonqualified plans		12 Benefits included in box 1	
13 See Instrs. for box 13		14 Other	

15 Statutory employee ☐ Deceased ☐ Pension plan ☐ Legal rep. ☐ Hshld. emp. ☐ Subtotal ☐ Deferred compensation ☐

16 State	Employer's state I.D. No.	17 State wages, tips, etc.	18 State income tax	19 Locality name	20 Local wages, tips, etc.	21 Local income tax
MA	041-327077	55,000	3,600			

Department of the Treasury—Internal Revenue Service

Form **W-2** Wage and Tax Statement 1997

This information is being furnished to the Internal Revenue Service.

Copy B To Be Filed With Employee's FEDERAL Tax Return

SCHEDULE K-1 (Form 1065)
Department of the Treasury
Internal Revenue Service

Partner's Share of Income, Credits, Deductions, etc.

▶ See separate instructions.

For calendar year 1997 or tax year beginning , 1997, and ending , 19

OMB No. 1545-0099

1997

Partner's identifying number ▶ 568-34-1110

Partnership's identifying number ▶ 55 : 1422327

Partner's name, address, and ZIP code

Scott Rucker
26 Willis Lane
Waltham, MA 02154

Partnership's name, address, and ZIP code

AutoProfit
100 Charles River
Cambridge, MA 02220

A This partner is a ☒ general partner ☐ limited partner ☐ limited liability company member

B What type of entity is this partner? ▶

C Is this partner a ☒ domestic or a ☐ foreign partner?

D Enter partner's percentage of:

	(i) Before change or termination	(ii) End of year
Profit sharing	%	20 %
Loss sharing	%	20 %
Ownership of capital	%	20 %

E IRS Center where partnership filed return: Andover, MA

F Partner's share of liabilities (see instructions):

Nonrecourse $ 0

Qualified nonrecourse financing $ 0

Other $ 20

G Tax shelter registration number ▶ N/A

H Check here if this partnership is a publicly traded partnership as defined in section 469(k)(2) ☐

I Check applicable boxes: (1) ☐ Final K-1 (2) ☐ Amended K-1

J **Analysis of partner's capital account:**

(a) Capital account at beginning of year	(b) Capital contributed during year	(c) Partner's share of lines 3, 4, and 7, Form 1065, Schedule M-2	(d) Withdrawals and distributions	(e) Capital account at end of year (combine columns (a) through (d))
23,000	0	(2700)	(0)	20,300

		(a) Distributive share item		(b) Amount	(c) 1040 filers enter the amount in column (b) on:
Income (Loss)	1	Ordinary income (loss) from trade or business activities	1	(2,700)	See page 6 of Partner's Instructions for Schedule K-1 (Form 1065).
	2	Net income (loss) from rental real estate activities	2		
	3	Net income (loss) from other rental activities	3		
	4	Portfolio income (loss):			
	a	Interest	4a		Sch. B, Part I, line 1
	b	Dividends	4b		Sch. B, Part II, line 5
	c	Royalties	4c		Sch. E, Part I, line 4
	d	Net short-term capital gain (loss)	4d		Sch. D, line 5, col. (f)
	e	Net long-term capital gain (loss):			
		(1) 28% rate gain (loss)	e(1)		Sch. D, line 12, col. (g)
		(2) Total for year	e(2)		Sch. D, line 12, col. (f)
	f	Other portfolio income (loss) *(attach schedule)*	4f		Enter on applicable line of your return.
	5	Guaranteed payments to partner	5		See page 6 of Partner's Instructions for Schedule K-1 (Form 1065).
	6	Net section 1231 gain (loss) (other than due to casualty or theft):			
	a	28% rate gain (loss)	6a		
	b	Total for year	6b		
	7	Other income (loss) *(attach schedule)*	7		Enter on applicable line of your return.
Deductions	8	Charitable contributions (see instructions) *(attach schedule)*	8	300	Sch. A, line 15 or 16
	9	Section 179 expense deduction	9		See page 7 of Partner's Instructions for Schedule K-1 (Form 1065).
	10	Deductions related to portfolio income *(attach schedule)*	10		
	11	Other deductions *(attach schedule)*	11		
Credits	12a	Low-income housing credit:			
		(1) From section 42(j)(5) partnerships for property placed in service before 1990	a(1)		Form 8586, line 5
		(2) Other than on line 12a(1) for property placed in service before 1990	a(2)		
		(3) From section 42(j)(5) partnerships for property placed in service after 1989	a(3)		
		(4) Other than on line 12a(3) for property placed in service after 1989	a(4)		
	b	Qualified rehabilitation expenditures related to rental real estate activities	12b		
	c	Credits (other than credits shown on lines 12a and 12b) related to rental real estate activities	12c		See page 8 of Partner's Instructions for Schedule K-1 (Form 1065).
	d	Credits related to other rental activities	12d		
	13	Other credits	13		

For Paperwork Reduction Act Notice, see Instructions for Form 1065. Cat. No. 11394R Schedule K-1 (Form 1065) 1997

	(a) Distributive share item		(b) Amount	(c) 1040 filers enter the amount in column (b) on:
Investment Interest	14a Interest expense on investment debts	14a		Form 4952, line 1
	b (1) Investment income included on lines 4a, 4b, 4c, and 4f	b(1)		See page 8 of Partner's Instructions for Schedule K-1 (Form 1065).
	(2) Investment expenses included on line 10	b(2)		
Self-employment	15a Net earnings (loss) from self-employment	15a	(2,700)	Sch. SE, Section A or B
	b Gross farming or fishing income	15b		See page 9 of Partner's Instructions for Schedule K-1 (Form 1065).
	c Gross nonfarm income	15c		
Adjustments and Tax Preference Items	16a Depreciation adjustment on property placed in service after 1986	16a		See page 9 of Partner's Instructions for Schedule K-1 (Form 1065) and Instructions for Form 6251.
	b Adjusted gain or loss	16b		
	c Depletion (other than oil and gas)	16c		
	d (1) Gross income from oil, gas, and geothermal properties	d(1)		
	(2) Deductions allocable to oil, gas, and geothermal properties	d(2)		
	e Other adjustments and tax preference items *(attach schedule)*	16e		
Foreign Taxes	17a Type of income ▶			Form 1116, check boxes
	b Name of foreign country or possession ▶			Form 1116, Part I
	c Total gross income from sources outside the United States *(attach schedule)*	17c		
	d Total applicable deductions and losses *(attach schedule)*	17d		
	e Total foreign taxes (check one): ▶ ☐ Paid ☐ Accrued	17e		Form 1116, Part II
	f Reduction in taxes available for credit *(attach schedule)*	17f		Form 1116, Part III
	g Other foreign tax information *(attach schedule)*	17g		See Instructions for Form 1116.
Other	18 Section 59(e)(2) expenditures: a Type ▶			See page 9 of Partner's Instructions for Schedule K-1 (Form 1065).
	b Amount	18b		
	19 Tax-exempt interest income	19		Form 1040, line 8b
	20 Other tax-exempt income	20		See page 9 of Partner's Instructions for Schedule K-1 (Form 1065).
	21 Nondeductible expenses	21		
	22 Distributions of money (cash and marketable securities)	22		
	23 Distributions of property other than money	23		
	24 Recapture of low-income housing credit:			
	a From section 42(j)(5) partnerships	24a		Form 8611, line 8
	b Other than on line 24a	24b		

Supplemental Information

25 Supplemental information required to be reported separately to each partner *(attach additional schedules if more space is needed)*:

Line 8 – 50% Limitation

REQUIREMENTS

Prepare the Rucker's 1997 federal income tax return, with supporting schedules and attachments. Use the following assumptions in preparing the return:

1. Use the whole dollar method for all forms.

2. Use all opportunities to minimize the 1997 federal income tax.

3. Disregard any possible penalties for underpayment of estimated taxes (Form 2210).

4. Do not prepare Form 6251 (Alternative Minimum Tax).

5. Do not prepare a state income tax return.

6. Not all information in the fact set has an impact on the final tax liability. However, the purpose of this project is to expose you to various aspects of tax law, not simply to get the correct tax liability. Therefore, when a form calls for information of the type provided in the fact set, complete the appropriate parts of the form even though the item may have no final effect on the tax liability. This includes the preparation of any worksheets suggested by the forms or instructions. For example, complete the medical expense deduction section of Schedule A, even though the medical expenses do no exceed 7.5% of Adjusted Gross Income.

7. Calculate tax liability using the 1997 Tax Rate Schedules, even if the instructions call for the use of the Tax Tables.

FORMS FOR INDIVIDUAL PRACTICE SET

Form **1040** Department of the Treasury — Internal Revenue Service

U.S. Individual Income Tax Return 1997

(99) IRS use only — Do not write or staple in this space.

For the year Jan 1 - Dec 31, 1997, or other tax year beginning , 1997, ending , 19 OMB No. 1545-0074

Label (See instructions.)

Use the IRS label. Otherwise, please print or type.

Your First Name	MI	Last Name	Your Social Security No.
If a Joint Return, Spouse's First Name	MI	Last Name	Spouse's Social Security No.
Home Address (number and street). If You Have a P.O. Box, See Instructions.		Apartment No.	**For help finding line instructions, see instructions in the booklet.**
City, Town or Post Office. If You Have a Foreign Address, See Instructions.		State ZIP Code	

Presidential Election Campaign (See instructions.)

	Yes	No	
Do you want $3 to go to this fund?			**Note:** *Checking 'Yes' will not change your tax or reduce your refund.*
If a joint return, does your spouse want $3 to go to this fund?			

Filing Status

Check only one box.

1 ☐ Single
2 ☐ Married filing joint return (even if only one had income)
3 ☐ Married filing separate return. Enter spouse's SSN above & full name here .... ►
4 ☐ Head of household (with qualifying person). (See instructions.) If the qualifying person is a child but not your dependent, enter this child's name here ... ►
5 ☐ Qualifying widow(er) with dependent child (year spouse died ► 19). (See instructions.)

Exemptions

6a ☐ **Yourself.** If your parent (or someone else) can claim you as a dependent on his or her tax return, **do not** check box 6a

b ☐ **Spouse**

No. of boxes checked on 6a and 6b ....

c **Dependents:**

(1) First name Last name	(2) Dependent's social security number	(3) Dependent's relationship to you	(4) No. of months lived in your home in 1997

If more than six dependents, see instructions.

No. of your children on 6c who:
- lived with you .....
- did not live with you due to divorce or separation (see instructions) ..

Dependents on line 6c not entered above ....

d Total number of exemptions claimed .... Add numbers entered on lines above . ►

Income

Attach Copy B of your Forms W-2, W-2G, & 1099-R here.

If you did not get a W-2, see instructions.

Enclose, but do not attach, any payment. Also, please use **Form 1040-V.**

7	Wages, salaries, tips, etc. Attach Form(s) W-2	7	
8a	**Taxable** interest. Attach Schedule B if required	8a	
b	**Tax-exempt** interest. **Do not** include on line 8a 8b		
9	Dividends. Attach Schedule B if required	9	
10	Taxable refunds, credits, or offsets of state and local income taxes (see instructions)	10	
11	Alimony received	11	
12	Business income or (loss). Attach Schedule C or C-EZ	12	
13	Capital gain or (loss). Attach Schedule D	13	
14	Other gains or (losses). Attach Form 4797	14	
15a	Total IRA distributions ...... 15a ; b Taxable amount (see instrs)	15b	
16a	Total pensions and annuities ..... 16a ; b Taxable amount (see instrs)	16b	
17	Rental real estate, royalties, partnerships, S corporations, trusts, etc. Attach Schedule E	17	
18	Farm income or (loss). Attach Schedule F	18	
19	Unemployment compensation	19	
20a	Social security benefits ...... 20a ; b Taxable amount (see instrs)	20b	
21	Other income. List type and amount — see instructions	21	
22	Add the amounts in the far right column for lines 7 - 21. This is your **total income** ...... ►	22	

Adjusted Gross Income

If line 32 is under $29,290 (under $9,770 if a child did not live with you), see EIC in the instructions.

23	IRA deduction (see instructions)	23			
24	Medical savings account deduction. Attach Form 8853	24			
25	Moving expenses. Attach Form 3903 or 3903-F	25			
26	One-half of self-employment tax. Attach Schedule SE	26			
27	Self-employed health insurance deduction (see instructions)	27			
28	Keogh and self-employed SEP and SIMPLE plans	28			
29	Penalty on early withdrawal of savings	29			
30a	Alimony paid. **b** Recipient's SSN ... ►	30a			
31	Add lines 23 - 30a			31	
32	Subtract line 31 from line 22. This is your **adjusted gross income** ►			32	

BAA For Privacy Act and Paperwork Reduction Act Notice, see instructions. Form **1040** (1997)

FDIA0112 12/10/97

Tax Computation

33 Amount from line 32 (adjusted gross income) 33

34a Check if: ☐ **You** were 65/older, ☐ Blind; ☐ **Spouse** was 65/older, ☐ Blind
Add the number of boxes checked above and enter the total here .... ► 34a

b If you are married filing separately and your spouse itemizes deductions or you were a dual-status alien, see instructions and check here .... ► 34b ☐

35 Enter the **larger** of your:
- **Itemized deductions** from Schedule A, line 28, **Or**
- **Standard deduction** shown below for your filing status. **But** see the instructions if you checked any box on line 34a or 34b **or** someone can claim you as a dependent.

• Single – $4,150 • Married filing jointly or Qualifying widow(er) – $6,900
• Head of household – $6,050 • Married filing separately – $3,450 35

36 Subtract line 35 from line 33 36

If you want the IRS to figure your tax, see instructions.

37 If line 33 is $90,900 or less, multiply $2,650 by the total number of exemptions claimed on line 6d. If line 33 is over $90,900, see the worksheet in the instructions for the amount to enter 37

38 **Taxable income.** Subtract line 37 from line 36. If line 37 is more than line 36, enter -0- 38

39 **Tax.** See instrs. Check if any tax from a ☐ Form(s) 8814 b ☐ Form 4972 .... ► 39

Credits

40 Credit for child and dependent care expenses. Attach Form 2441 40
41 Credit for the elderly or the disabled. Attach Sch R 41
42 Adoption credit. Attach Form 8839 42
43 Foreign tax credit. Attach Form 1116 43
44 Other. Check if from .... a ☐ Form 3800 b ☐ Form 8396 c ☐ Form 8801 d ☐ Form (specify) ______ 44
45 Add lines 40 through 44 45
46 Subtract line 45 from line 39. If line 45 is more than line 39, enter -0- .... ► 46

Other Taxes

47 Self-employment tax. Attach Schedule SE 47
48 Alternative minimum tax. Attach Form 6251 48
49 SS and Medicare tax on tip income not reported to employer. Attach Form 4137 49
50 Tax on qualified retirement plans (including IRAs) and MSAs. Attach Form 5329 if required 50
51 Advance earned income credit payments from Form(s) W-2 51
52 Household employment taxes. Attach Schedule H 52
53 Add lns 46 - 52. This is your **total tax** .... ► 53

Payments

54 Federal income tax withheld from Forms W-2 and 1099 54
55 1997 estimated tax payments and amount applied from 1996 return 55
56a **Earned income credit.** Attach Schedule EIC if you have a qualifying child. **b** Nontaxable earned income: amount .. ► ______ and type ... ► ______ 56a

No

Attach Forms W-2, W-2G, and 1099-R to page 1.

57 Amount paid with Form 4868 (request for extension) 57
58 Excess social security and RRTA tax withheld (see instrs) 58
59 Other payments. Check if from ..... a ☐ Form 2439 b ☐ Form 4136 59
60 Add lines 54, 55, 56a, 57, 58, and 59. These are your **total payments** .... ► 60

Refund

Have it directly deposited! See instructions and fill in 62b, 62c, and 62d.

61 If line 60 is more than line 53, subtract line 53 from line 60. This is the amount you **Overpaid** 61
62a Amount of line 61 you want **Refunded to You** .... ► 62a
► b Routing number .. ______ c Type: ☐ Checking ☐ Savings
► d Account number .. ______
63 Amount of line 61 you want **Applied to Your 1998 Estimated Tax** .... ► 63

Amount You Owe

64 If line 53 is more than line 60, subtract line 60 from line 53. This is the **Amount You Owe.** For details on how to pay, see instructions .... ► 64
65 Estimated tax penalty. Also include on line 64 65

Sign Here

Under penalties of perjury, I declare that I have examined this return and accompanying schedules and statements, and to the best of my knowledge and belief, they are true, correct, and complete. Declaration of preparer (other than taxpayer) is based on all information of which preparer has any knowledge.

Keep a copy of this return for your records.

Your Signature	Date	Your Occupation
►		
Spouse's Signature. If a Joint Return, BOTH Must Sign.	Date	Spouse's Occupation
►		

Paid Preparer's Use Only

	Date	Check if self-employed ☐	Preparer's Social Security No.
Preparer's Signature ►			
Firm's Name (or yours if self-employed) and Address ► Self-prepared		EIN	
		ZIP Code	

Schedule A
(Form 1040)

Department of the Treasury
Internal Revenue Service (99)

Itemized Deductions

► **Attach to Form 1040.**
► **See Instructions for Schedule A (Form 1040).**

OMB No. 1545-0074

1997

07

Name(s) Shown on Form 1040

Your Social Security Number

Medical and Dental Expenses		**Caution:** *Do not include expenses reimbursed or paid by others.*			
	1	Medical and dental expenses (see instructions)	1		
	2	Enter amount from Form 1040, line 33 2			
	3	Multiply line 2 above by 7.5% (.075)	3		
	4	Subtract line 3 from line 1. If line 3 is more than line 1, enter -0-		4	
Taxes You Paid (See instructions.)	5	State and local income taxes	5		
	6	Real estate taxes (see instructions)	6		
	7	Personal property taxes	7		
	8	Other taxes. List type and amount ►	8		
	9	Add lines 5 through 8		9	
Interest You Paid (See instructions.)	10	Home mortgage interest and points reported to you on Form 1098	10		
	11	Home mortgage interest not reported to you on Form 1098. If paid to the person from whom you bought the home, see instructions and show that person's name, identifying number, and address ►	11		
Note: Personal interest is not deductible.	12	Points not reported to you on Form 1098. See instructions for special rules	12		
	13	Investment interest. Attach Form 4952 if required. (See instructions.)	13		
	14	Add lines 10 through 13		14	
Gifts to Charity	15	Gifts by cash or check. If you made any gift of $250 or more, see instructions	15		
If you made a gift and got a benefit for it, see instructions.	16	Other than by cash or check. If any gift of $250 or more, see instructions. You **Must** attach Form 8283 if over $500	16		
	17	Carryover from prior year	17		
	18	Add lines 15 through 17		18	
Casualty and Theft Losses	19	Casualty or theft loss(es). Attach Form 4684. (See instructions.)		19	
Job Expenses and Most Other Miscellaneous Deductions	20	Unreimbursed employee expenses — job travel, union dues, job education, etc. You **Must** attach Form 2106 or 2106-EZ if required (See instructions.) ►	20		
	21	Tax preparation fees	21		
(See instructions for expenses to deduct here.)	22	Other expenses — investment, safe deposit box, etc. List type and amount ►	22		
	23	Add lines 20 through 22	23		
	24	Enter amount from Form 1040, line 33 24			
	25	Multiply line 24 above by 2% (.02)	25		
	26	Subtract line 25 from line 23. If line 25 is more than line 23, enter -0-		26	
Other Miscellaneous Deductions	27	Other — from list in the instructions. List type and amount ►		27	
Total Itemized Deductions	28	Is Form 1040, line 33, over $121,200 (over $60,600 if married filing separately)?			
		No. Your deduction is not limited. Add the amounts in the far right column for lines 4 through 27. Also, enter on Form 1040, line 35, the **larger** of this amount or your standard deduction. ►		28	
		Yes. Your deduction may be limited. See instructions for the amount to enter.			

Name(s) Shown on Form 1040. Do Not Enter Name and Social Security Number if Shown on Schedule A. | **Your Social Security Number**

Schedule B — Interest and Dividend Income

08

Part I Interest Income

(See instructions.)

Note: If you received a Form 1099-INT, Form 1099-OID, or substitute statement from a brokerage firm, list the firm's name as the payer and enter the total interest shown on that form.

Note: *If you had over $400 in taxable interest income, you must also complete Part III.*

			Amount
1	List name of payer. If any interest is from a seller-financed mortgage and the buyer used the property as a personal residence, see the instructions and list this interest first. Also, show that buyer's social security number and address ►	1	
2	Add the amounts on line 1	2	
3	Excludable interest on series EE U.S. savings bonds issued after 1989 from Form 8815, line 14. You **must** attach Form 8815 to Form 1040	3	
4	Subtract line 3 from line 2. Enter the result here and on Form 1040, line 8a ►	4	

Part II Dividend Income

(See instructions.)

Note: If you received a Form 1099-DIV, or substitute statement from a brokerage firm, list the firm's name as the payer and enter the total dividends shown on that form.

Note: *If you had over $400 in gross dividends and/or other distributions on stock, you must also complete Part III.*

					Amount
5	List name of payer. Include gross dividends and/or other distributions on stock here. Any capital gain distributions and nontaxable distributions will be deducted on lines 7 and 8 ►			5	
6	Add the amounts on line 5			6	
7	Capital gain distributions. Enter here and on Schedule D	7			
8	Nontaxable distributions. (See the instructions for Form 1040, line 9.)	8			
9	Add lines 7 and 8			9	
10	Subtract line 9 from line 6. Enter the result here and on Form 1040, line 9 ►			10	

Part III Foreign Accounts and Trusts

(See instructions.)

	You must complete this part if you **(a)** had over $400 of interest or dividends; **(b)** had a foreign account; or **(c)** received a distribution from, or were a grantor of, or a transferor to, a foreign trust.	Yes	No
11 a	At any time during 1997, did you have an interest in or a signature or other authority over a financial account in a foreign country, such as a bank account, securities account, or other financial account? See instructions for exceptions and filing requirements for Form TD F 90-22.1		
b	If 'yes,' enter the name of the foreign country ►		
12	During 1997, did you receive a distribution from, or were you the grantor of, or transferor to, a foreign trust? If 'yes,' you may have to file Form 3520 or 926. See instructions		

Schedule C (Form 1040)

Department of the Treasury Internal Revenue Service (99)

Profit or Loss from Business
(Sole Proprietorship)

► Partnerships, joint ventures, etc, must file Form 1065.
► Attach to Form 1040 or Form 1041. ► See instructions for Schedule C (Form 1040).

OMB No. 1545-0074

1997

09

Name of Proprietor | **Social Security Number (SSN)**

A Principal Business or Profession, Including Product or Service (see instructions) | **B Enter Principal Business Code (see instr)** ►

C Business Name. If No Separate Business Name, Leave Blank. | **D Employer ID No. (EIN), if Any**

E Business Addr (include suite or room no.) City, Town or P.O., State, & ZIP Code ►

F Accounting method: **(1)** ☐ Cash **(2)** ☐ Accrual **(3)** ☐ Other (specify) ►

G Did you 'materially participate' in the operation of this business during 1997? If 'No,' see instructions for limit on losses ☐ **Yes** ☐ **No**

H If you started or acquired this business during 1997, check here ► ☐

Part I Income

1	Gross receipts or sales. **Caution:** *If this income was reported to you on Form W-2 and the 'Statutory employee' box on that form was checked, see the instructions and check here* ► ☐	1	
2	Returns and allowances	2	
3	Subtract line 2 from line 1	3	
4	Cost of goods sold (from line 42 on page 2)	4	
5	**Gross profit**. Subtract line 4 from line 3	5	
6	Other income, including federal and state gasoline or fuel tax credit or refund	6	
7	**Gross income**. Add lines 5 and 6 ►	7	

Part II Expenses. Enter expenses for business use of your home **only** on line 30.

8	Advertising	8		19	Pension and profit-sharing plans	19	
9	Bad debts from sales or services (see instructions)	9		20	Rent or lease (see instructions):		
				a	Vehicles, machinery, and equipment	20a	
10	Car and truck expenses (see instrs)	10		b	Other business property	20b	
11	Commissions and fees	11		21	Repairs and maintenance	21	
12	Depletion	12		22	Supplies (not included in Part III)	22	
13	Depreciation and section 179 expense deduction (not included in Part III) (see instructions)	13		23	Taxes and licenses	23	
				24	Travel, meals, and entertainment:		
				a	Travel	24a	
14	Employee benefit programs (other than on line 19)	14		b	Meals and entertainment		
15	Insurance (other than health)	15		c	Enter 50% of line 24b subject to limitations (see instrs)		
16	Interest:						
a	Mortgage (paid to banks, etc)	16a		d	Subtract line 24c from line 24b	24d	
b	Other	16b		25	Utilities	25	
17	Legal and professional services	17		26	Wages (less employment credits)	26	
18	Office expense	18		27	Other expenses (from line 48 on page 2)	27	

28	**Total expenses** before expenses for business use of home. Add lines 8 through 27 in columns ►	28	
29	Tentative profit (loss). Subtract line 28 from line 7	29	
30	Expenses for business use of your home. Attach **Form 8829**	30	
31	**Net profit or (loss).** Subtract line 30 from line 29. • If a profit, enter on **Form 1040, line 12**, and **also** on **Schedule SE, line 2** (statutory employees, see instructions). Estates and trusts, enter on Form 1041, line 3 • If a loss, you **must** go on to line 32	31	
32	If you have a loss, check the box that describes your investment in this activity (see instructions). • If you checked 32a, enter the loss on **Form 1040, line 12**, and **also** on **Schedule SE, line 2** (statutory employees, see instructions). Estates and trusts, enter on Form 1041, line 3 • If you checked 32b, you **must** attach **Form 6198**	32a ☐ All investment is at risk. 32b ☐ Some investment is not at risk.	

Part III Cost of Goods Sold (See instructions)

33 Method(s) used to value closing inventory: **a** ☐ Cost **b** ☐ Lower of cost or market **c** ☐ Other (attach explanation)

34 Was there any change in determining quantities, costs, or valuations between opening and closing inventory? If 'Yes,' attach explanation . . . ☐ **Yes** ☐ **No**

35 Inventory at beginning of year. If different from last year's closing inventory, attach explanation	**35**	
36 Purchases less cost of items withdrawn for personal use	**36**	
37 Cost of labor. Do not include salary paid to yourself	**37**	
38 Materials and supplies	**38**	
39 Other costs	**39**	
40 Add lines 35 through 39	**40**	
41 Inventory at end of year	**41**	
42 **Cost of goods sold.** Subtract line 41 from line 40. Enter the result here and on page 1, line 4	**42**	

Part IV Information on Your Vehicle.

Complete this part **Only** if you are claiming car or truck expenses on line 10 and are not required to file Form 4562 for this business. See the instructions for line 13 to find out if you must file.

43 When did you place your vehicle in service for business purposes? (month, day, year) ► ____________

44 Of the total number of miles you drove your vehicle during 1997, enter the number of miles you used your vehicle for:

a Business ____________ **b** Commuting ____________ **c** Other ____________

45 Do you (or your spouse) have another vehicle available for personal use? . . . ☐ **Yes** ☐ **No**

46 Was your vehicle available for use during off-duty hours? . . . ☐ **Yes** ☐ **No**

47a Do you have evidence to support your deduction? . . . ☐ **Yes** ☐ **No**

b If 'Yes,' is the evidence written? . . . ☐ **Yes** ☐ **No**

Part V Other Expenses.

List below business expenses not included on lines 8 - 26 or line 30.

48 **Total other expenses.** Enter here and on page 1, line 27	**48**	

Schedule D (Form 1040)

Department of the Treasury
Internal Revenue Service

Capital Gains and Losses

► Attach to Form 1040. ► See instructions for Schedule D (Form 1040).
► Use Schedule D-1 for more space to list transactions for lines 1 and 8.

OMB No. 1545-0074

1997

12

Name(s) Shown on Form 1040 | **Your Social Security Number**

Part I Short-Term Capital Gains and Losses – Assets Held One Year or Less

(a) Description of property (Example: 100 shares 'XYZ' Co)	(b) Date acquired (Mo, day, yr)	(c) Date sold (Mo, day, yr)	(d) Sales price	(e) Cost or other basis	(f) GAIN or (LOSS) FOR ENTIRE YEAR. Subtract (e) from (d)
1					
2 Enter your short-term totals, if any, from Schedule D-1, line 2 2					
3 **Total short-term sales price amounts.** Add column (d) of lines 1 and 2 3					
4 Short-term gain from Forms 2119 and 6252, and short-term gain or (loss) from Forms 4684, 6781, and 8824 4					
5 Net short-term gain or (loss) from partnerships, S corporations, estates, and trusts from Schedule(s) K-1 5					
6 Short-term capital loss carryover. Enter the amount, if any, from line 9 of your 1996 Capital Loss Carryover Worksheet 6					
7 **Net short-term capital gain or (loss).** Combine lines 1 through 6 in column (f) .... ► 7					

Part II Long-Term Capital Gains and Losses – Assets Held More Than One Year

(a) Description of property (Example: 100 shares 'XYZ' Co)	(b) Date acquired (Mo, day, yr)	(c) Date sold (Mo, day, yr)	(d) Sales price	(e) Cost or other basis	(f) GAIN or (LOSS) FOR ENTIRE YEAR. Subtract (e) from (d)	(g) 28% RATE GAIN or (LOSS) * (see instructions)
8						
9 Enter your long-term totals, if any, from Schedule D-1, line 9 9						
10 **Total long-term sales price amounts.** Add column (d) of lines 8 and 9 10						
11 Gain from Form 4797, Part I; long-term gain from Forms 2119, 2439, and 6252; and long-term gain or (loss) from Forms 4684, 6781, and 8824 11						
12 Net long-term gain or (loss) from partnerships, S corporations, estates, and trusts from Schedule(s) K-1 12						
13 Capital gain distributions 13						
14 Long-term capital loss carryover. Enter in both columns (f) and (g) the amount, if any, from line 14 of your 1996 Capital Loss Carryover Worksheet 14						
15 Combine lines 8 through 14 in column (g) 15						
16 **Net long-term capital gain or (loss).** Combine lines 8 through 14 in column (f) .... ► 16						

***28% Rate Gain or Loss** includes all gains and losses in Part II, column (f) from sales, exchanges, or conversions (including installment payments received) **either:**
- **Before** May 7, 1997, **or**
- **After** July 28, 1997, for assets held more than 1 year but **not** more than 18 months.

It also includes **All** 'collectibles gains and losses' (as defined in the instructions).

Part III Summary of Parts I and II

17 Combine lines 7 and 16. If a loss, go to line 18. If a gain, enter the gain on Form 1040, line 13 . . . **17**

Next: Complete Form 1040 through line 38. Then, go to **Part IV** to figure your tax if:

- Both lines 16 and 17 are gains, **and,**
- Form 1040, line 38, is more than zero.

18 If line 17 is a loss, enter here and as a (loss) on Form 1040, line 13, the **smaller** of these losses:

- The loss on line 17; **or**
- ($3,000) or, if married filing separately, ($1,500) . . . **18**

Next: Complete Form 1040 through line 36. Then, complete the **Capital Loss Carryover Worksheet** if:

- The loss on line 17 exceeds the loss on line 18, **or**
- Form 1040, line 36, is a loss.

Part IV Tax Computation Using Maximum Capital Gains Rates

19	Enter your taxable income from Form 1040, line 38		19	
20	Enter the **smaller** of line 16 or line 17	20		
21	If you are filing Form 4952, enter the amount from Form 4952, line 4e	21		
22	Subtract line 21 from line 20. If zero or less, enter -0-	22		
23	Combine lines 7 and 15. If zero or less, enter -0-	23		
24	Enter the **smaller** of line 15 or line 23, but not less than zero	24		
25	Enter your unrecaptured section 1250 gain, if any (see instructions)	25		
26	Add lines 24 and 25	26		
27	Subtract line 26 from line 22. If zero or less, enter -0-		27	
28	Subtract line 27 from line 19. If zero or less, enter -0-		28	
29	Enter the **smaller** of line 19 or $41,200 ($24,650 if single; $20,600 if married filing separately; $33,050 if head of household)		29	
30	Enter the **smaller** of line 28 or line 29		30	
31	Subtract line 22 from line 19. If zero or less, enter -0-		31	
32	Enter the **larger** of line 30 or line 31		32	
33	Figure the tax on the amount on line 32. Use the Tax Table or Tax Rate Schedules, whichever applies ►		33	
34	Enter the amount from line 29		34	
35	Enter the amount from line 28		35	
36	Subtract line 35 from line 34. If zero or less, enter -0-		36	
37	Multiply line 36 by 10% (.10) ►		37	
38	Enter the **smaller** of line 19 or line 27		38	
39	Enter the amount from line 36		39	
40	Subtract line 39 from line 38. If zero or less, enter -0-		40	
41	Multiply line 40 by 20% (.20) ►		41	
42	Enter the **smaller** of line 22 or line 25		42	
43	Add lines 22 and 32	43		
44	Enter the amount from line 19	44		
45	Subtract line 44 from line 43. If zero or less, enter -0-		45	
46	Subtract line 45 from line 42. If zero or less, enter -0-		46	
47	Multiply line 46 by 25% (.25) ►		47	
48	Enter the amount from line 19		48	
49	Add lines 32, 36, 40, and 46		49	
50	Subtract line 49 from line 48		50	
51	Multiply line 50 by 28% (.28) ►		51	
52	Add lines 33, 37, 41, 47, and 51		52	
53	Figure the tax on the amount on line 19. Use the Tax Table or Tax Rate Schedules, whichever applies		53	
54	**Tax.** Enter the **smaller** of line 52 or line 53 here and on Form 1040, line 39 ►		54	

Schedule E (Form 1040)

Department of the Treasury Internal Revenue Service (99)

Supplemental Income and Loss

(From rental real estate, royalties, partnerships, S corporations, estates, trusts, REMICs, etc)

► Attach to Form 1040 or Form 1041.

► See instructions for Schedule E (Form 1040).

OMB No. 1545-0074

1997

13

Name(s) Shown on Return

Your Social Security Number

Part I Income or Loss from Rental Real Estate and Royalties

Note: *Report income and expenses from your business of renting personal property on **Schedule C** or **C-EZ**. Report farm rental income or loss from **Form 4835** on page 2, line 39.*

1	Show the kind and location of each **rental real estate property:**
A	
B	
C	

2 For each rental real estate property listed on line 1, did you or your family use it during the tax year for personal purposes for more than the greater of:

- 14 days, **or**
- 10% of the total days rented at fair rental value?

(See instructions.)

	Yes	No
A		
B		
C		

		Properties A	Properties B	Properties C		Totals (Add columns A, B, and C.)
Income:						
3 Rents received	3				3	
4 Royalties received	4				4	
Expenses:						
5 Advertising	5					
6 Auto and travel (see instructions)	6					
7 Cleaning and maintenance	7					
8 Commissions	8					
9 Insurance	9					
10 Legal and other professional fees	10					
11 Management fees	11					
12 Mortgage interest paid to banks, etc (see instructions)	12				12	
13 Other interest	13					
14 Repairs	14					
15 Supplies	15					
16 Taxes	16					
17 Utilities	17					
18 Other (list) ►	18					
19 Add lines 5 through 18	19				19	
20 Depreciation expense or depletion (see instructions)	20				20	
21 Total expenses. Add lines 19 and 20	21					
22 Income or (loss) from rental real estate or royalty properties. Subtract line 21 from line 3 (rents) or line 4 (royalties). If the result is a (loss), see instructions to find out if you must file **Form 6198**	22					
23 Deductible rental real estate loss. **Caution:** *Your rental real estate loss on line 22 may be limited. See instructions to find out if you must file **Form 8582**. Real estate professionals must complete line 42 on page 2*	23					

24 **Income**. Add positive amounts shown on line 22. **Do not** include any losses	24	
25 **Losses.** Add royalty losses from line 22 and rental real estate losses from line 23. Enter total losses here	25	
26 Total rental real estate and royalty income or (loss). Combine lines 24 and 25. Enter the result here. If Parts II, III, IV, and line 39 on page 2 do not apply to you, also enter this amount on Form 1040, line 17. Otherwise, include this amount in the total on line 40 on page 2	26	

Name(s) Shown on Return. Do Not Enter Name and Social Security Number if Shown on Page 1. | Your Social Security Number

Note: *If you report amounts from farming or fishing on Schedule E, you must enter your gross income from those activities on line 41 below. Real estate professionals must complete line 42 below.*

Part II Income or Loss from Partnerships and S Corporations

Note: *If you report a loss from an at-risk activity, you* **must** *check either column* **(e)** *or* **(f)** *on line 27 to describe your investment in the activity. See instructions. If you check column* **(f)**, *you must attach* **Form 6198.**

27	**(a)** Name	**(b)** Enter **P** for partnership; **S** for S Corporation	**(c)** Check if foreign partnership	**(d)** Employer identification number	Investment at Risk? **(e)** All is at risk	**(f)** Some is not at risk
A						
B						
C						
D						
E						

	Passive Income and Loss		Nonpassive Income and Loss		
	(g) Passive loss allowed (attach **Form 8582** if required)	**(h)** Passive income from **Schedule K-1**	**(i)** Nonpassive loss from **Schedule K-1**	**(j)** Section 179 expense deduction from **Form 4562**	**(k)** Nonpassive income from **Schedule K-1**
A					
B					
C					
D					
E					
28a Totals					
b Totals					

29	Add columns (h) and (k) of line 28a	29	
30	Add columns (g), (i), and (j) of line 28b	30	
31	Total partnership and S corporation income or (loss). Combine lines 29 and 30. Enter the result here and include in the total on line 40 below	31	

Part III Income or Loss from Estates and Trusts

32	**(a)** Name	**(b)** Employer ID no.
A		
B		

	Passive Income and Loss		Nonpassive Income and Loss	
	(c) Passive deduction or loss allowed (attach **Form 8582** if required)	**(d)** Passive income from **Schedule K-1**	**(e)** Deduction or loss from **Schedule K-1**	**(f)** Other income from **Schedule K-1**
A				
B				
33a Totals				
b Totals				

34	Add columns (d) and (f) of line 33a	34	
35	Add columns (c) and (e) of line 33b	35	
36	Total estate and trust income or (loss). Combine lines 34 and 35. Enter the result here and include in the total on line 40 below	36	

Part IV Income or Loss from Real Estate Mortgage Investment Conduits (REMICs) – Residual Holder

37	**(a)** Name	**(b)** Employer identification number	**(c)** Excess inclusion from **Schedules Q,** line 2c (see instructions)	**(d)** Taxable income (net loss) from **Schedules Q,** line 1b	**(e)** Income from **Schedules Q,** line 3b

38	Combine columns (d) and (e) only. Enter the result here and include in the total on line 40 below	38	

Part V Summary

39	Net farm rental income or (loss) from **Form 4835**. Also, complete line 41 below			39	
40	**Total** income or (loss). Combine lines 26, 31, 36, 38, and 39. Enter the result here and on Form 1040, line 17 ►			40	
41	**Reconciliation of Farming and Fishing Income:** Enter your **gross** farming and fishing income reported on Form 4835, line 7; Schedule K-1 (Form 1065), line 15b; Schedule K-1 (Form 1120S), line 23; and Schedule K-1 (Form 1041), line 14 (see instructions)	41			
42	**Reconciliation for Real Estate Professionals.** If you were a real estate professional (see instructions), enter the net income or (loss) you reported anywhere on Form 1040 from all rental real estate activities in which you materially participated under the passive activity loss rules	42			

Schedule SE
(Form 1040)

Department of the Treasury
Internal Revenue Service (99)

Self-Employment Tax

► **Attach to Form 1040.**
► **See instructions for Schedule SE (Form 1040).**

OMB No. 1545-0074

1997

17

Name of Person with **Self-Employment** Income (as shown on Form 1040)	Social Security Number of Person with **Self-Employment** Income ►	

Who Must File Schedule SE

You must file Schedule SE if:

- You had net earnings from self-employment from **other than** church employee income (line 4 of Short Schedule SE or line 4c of Long Schedule SE) of $400 or more, **Or**
- You had church employee income of $108.28 or more. Income from services you performed as a minister or a member of a religious order **is not** church employee income. See instructions.

Note: *Even if you have a loss or a small amount of income from self-employment, it may be to your benefit to file Schedule SE and use either 'optional method' in Part II of Long Schedule SE. See instructions.*

Exception: If your only self-employment income was from earnings as a minister, member of a religious order, or Christian Science practitioner, **and** you filed Form 4361 and received IRS approval not to be taxed on those earnings, **do not** file Schedule SE. Instead, write 'Exempt – Form 4361' on Form 1040, line 47.

May I Use Short Schedule SE or Must I Use Long Schedule SE?

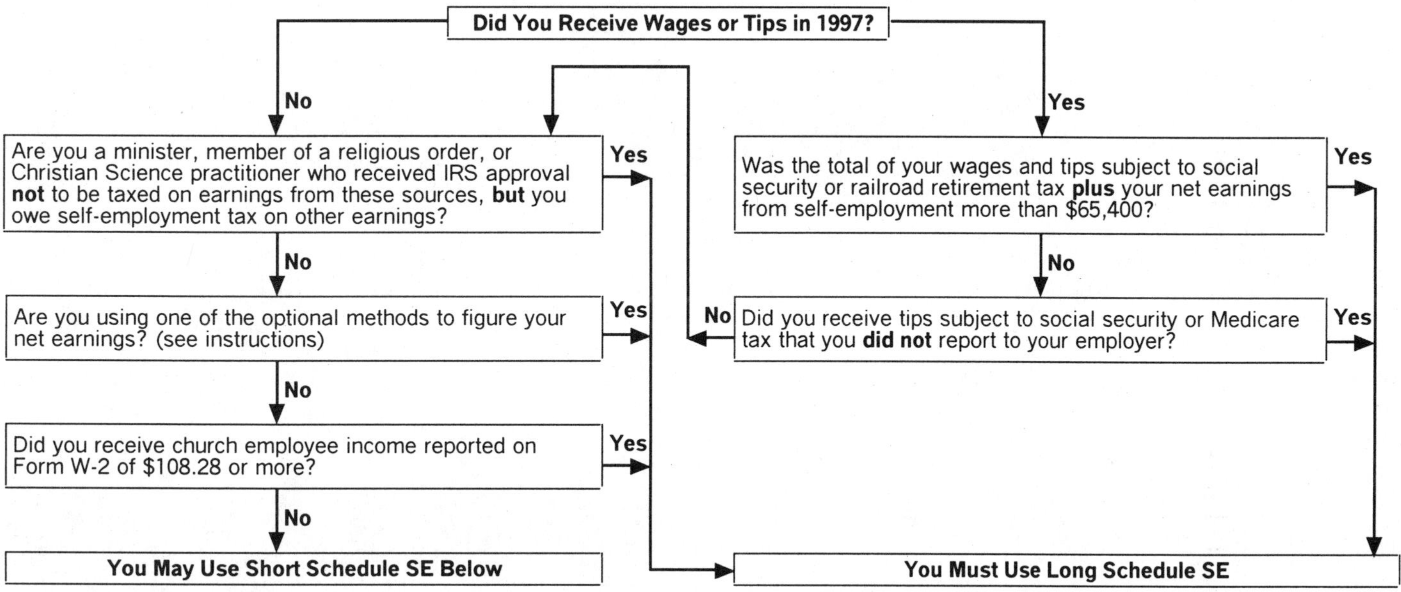

Section A – Short Schedule SE. Caution: *Read above to see if you can use Short Schedule SE.*

1	Net farm profit or (loss) from Schedule F, line 36, and farm partnerships, Schedule K-1 (Form 1065), line 15a	1	
2	Net profit or (loss) from Schedule C, line 31; Schedule C-EZ, line 3; and Schedule K-1 (Form 1065), line 15a (other than farming). Ministers and members of religious orders, see instructions for amounts to report on this line. See instructions for other income to report	2	
3	Combine lines 1 and 2	3	
4	**Net earnings from self-employment.** Multiply line 3 by 92.35% (.9235). If less than $400, **do not** file this schedule; you do not owe self-employment tax ►	4	
5	**Self-employment tax.** If the amount on line 4 is: • $65,400 or less, multiply line 4 by 15.3% (.153). Enter the result here and on **Form 1040, line 47.** • More than $65,400, multiply line 4 by 2.9% (.029). Then, add $8,109.60 to the result. Enter the total here and on **Form 1040, line 47.**	5	
6	**Deduction for one-half of self-employment tax.** Multiply line 5 by 50% (.5). Enter the result here and on **Form 1040, line 26** — 6		

Form **2119**

Department of the Treasury
Internal Revenue Service

Sale of Your Home

► Attach to Form 1040 for year of sale.
► See separate instructions. ► Please print or type.

OMB No. 1545-0072

1997
20

Your First Name and Initial. If a Joint Return, Also Give Spouse's Name and Initial.	Last Name	Your Social Security Number
If you are filing this form by itself and not with your tax return, see instructions. Present Address (no., street, and apt no., rural route, or P.O. box no. if mail is not delivered to street address)		Spouse's Social Security Number
City, Town or Post Office	State ZIP Code	

Part I Gain on Sale

1 Date your former main home was sold. If sold after May 6, 1997, see instructions ► **1** ______ month day year

2 Have you bought or built a new main home? ☐ Yes ☐ No

3 If any part of either main home was ever rented out or used for business, check here ► ☐ and see instructions.

4	Selling price of home. Do not include personal property items you sold with your home	**4**	
5	Expense of sale	**5**	
6	Subtract line 5 from line 4	**6**	
7	Adjusted basis of home sold	**7**	
8	**Gain on sale.** Subtract line 7 from line 6. **If zero or less, stop** and attach this form to your return	**8**	

- For sales **before May 7, 1997,** you must go to Part II or Part III, whichever applies. **But** if line 2 is 'No,' go to line 9.
- For sales **after May 6, 1997,** you must go to Part IV on page 2 to figure any exclusion. **But** if you qualify and elect to use the rules for sales before May 7, 1997, go to Part II or Part III, whichever applies.

9 If you haven't replaced your home, do you plan to do so within the **replacement period**? ☐ Yes ☐ No

- If line 9 is 'Yes,' stop here, attach this form to your return, and see **Additional filing requirements** in the instructions.
- If line 9 is 'No', you **must** go to Part II or Part III, whichever applies.

Part II One-Time Exclusion of Gain for People Age 55 or Older — By completing this part, you are electing to take the one-time exclusion. If you are not electing to take the exclusion, go to Part III now.

10 Who was age 55 or older on the date of sale? ☐ You ☐ Your spouse ☐ Both of you

11 Did the person who was 55 or older own and use the property as his or her main home for a total of at least 3 years of the 5-year period before the sale? See instructions for exceptions. If 'No', go to Part III now ☐ Yes ☐ No

12 At the time of sale, who owned the home? ☐ You ☐ Your spouse ☐ Both of you

13	Social security number of spouse at the time of sale if you had a different spouse from the one above. If you were not married at the time of sale, enter 'None' ►	**13**	
14	**Exclusion.** Enter the **smaller** of line 8 or $125,000 ($62,500 if married filing separate return). Then, go to line 15	**14**	

Part III Adjusted Sales Price, Taxable Gain, and Adjusted Basis of New Home

15 If line 14 is blank, enter the amount from line 8. Otherwise, subtract line 14 from line 8 **15** ______

- If line 15 is zero, stop and attach this form to your return.
- If line 15 is more than zero and line 2 is 'Yes', go to line 16 now.
- If you are reporting this sale on the installment method, stop and see the instructions.
- All others, stop and **enter the amount from line 15 on Schedule D, line 4 or line 11.**

16	Fixing-up expenses (see instructions for time limits)	**16**	
17	If line 14 is blank, enter amount from line 16. Otherwise, add lines 14 and 16	**17**	
18	**Adjusted sales price.** Subtract line 17 from line 6	**18**	
19a	Date you moved into new home ► ______ **b** Cost of new home	**19b**	
20	Subtract line 19b from line 18. If zero or less, enter -0-	**20**	
21	**Taxable gain.** Enter the **smaller** of line 15 or line 20	**21**	

- If line 21 is zero, go to line 22 and attach this form to your return.
- If you are reporting this sale on the installment method, see the line 15 instructions and go to line 22.
- All others, **enter the amount from line 21 on Schedule D, line 4 or line 11,** and go to line 22.

22	Postponed gain. Subtract line 21 from line 15	**22**	
23	**Adjusted basis of new home.** Subtract line 22 from line 19b	**23**	

Part IV Exclusion and Taxable Gain for Sales After May 6, 1997

24 Did you (or your spouse if filing a joint return) own and use the property as your main home for a total of at least 2 years of the 5-year period before the sale? See instructions for exceptions ☐ Yes ☐ No

25	Maximum exclusion. See instructions for the amount to enter	**25**	
26	Enter the amount from line 8	**26**	
27	**Exclusion.** Enter the **smaller** of line 25 or line 26. If line 26 is the smaller amount, stop and attach this form to your return. Otherwise, go to line 28	**27**	
28	**Taxable gain.** Subtract line 27 from line 26	**28**	

- If you are reporting this sale on the installment method, see the line 15 instructions.
- All others, enter the amount from line 28 on **Schedule D, line 4 or line 11.**

Sign here only if you are filing this form by itself and not with your tax return.

Under penalties of perjury, I declare that I have examined this form, including attachments, and to the best of my knowledge and belief, it is true, correct, and complete.

Your Signature	Date	Spouse's Signature	Date
►		►	

If a joint return, both must sign.

Form **4684**

Department of the Treasury
Internal Revenue Service

Casualties and Thefts

▸ See separate instructions.
▸ Attach to your tax return.
▸ Use a separate Form 4684 for each different casualty or theft.

OMB No. 1545-0177

1997

26

Name(s) Shown on Tax Return | Identifying Number

Section A – Personal Use Property (Use this section to report casualties and thefts of property **not** used in a trade or business or for income-producing purposes.)

1 Description of properties (show type, location, and date acquired for each):

Property **A** ______

Property **B** ______

Property **C** ______

Property **D** ______

		Properties (Use a separate column for each property lost or damaged from one casualty or theft.)			
		A	B	C	D
2 Cost or other basis of each property	2				
3 Insurance or other reimbursement (whether or not you filed a claim). See instructions	3				
Note: *If line 2 is* **more than** *line 3, skip line 4.* 4 Gain from casualty or theft. If line 3 is **more than** line 2, enter the difference here and skip lines 5 through 9 for that column. See instructions if line 3 includes insurance or other reimbursement you did not claim, or you received payment for your loss in a later tax year	4				
5 Fair market value **before** casualty or theft	5				
6 Fair market value **after** casualty or theft	6				
7 Subtract line 6 from line 5	7				
8 Enter the **smaller** of line 2 or line 7	8				
9 Subtract line 3 from line 8. If zero or less, enter -0-	9				

10 Casualty or theft loss. Add the amounts on line 9. Enter the total	10	
11 Enter the amount from line 10 or $100, whichever is **smaller**	11	
12 Subtract line 11 from line 10	12	
Caution: *Use only one Form 4684 for lines 13 through 18.*		
13 Add the amounts on line 12 of all Forms 4684	13	
14 Combine the amounts from line 4 of all Forms 4684	14	
15 • If line 14 is **more than** line 13, enter the difference here and on Schedule D. Do not complete the rest of this section (see instructions). • If line 14 is **less than** line 13, enter -0- here and continue with the form. • If line 14 is **equal to** line 13, enter -0- here. Do not complete the rest of this section.	15	
16 If line 14 is **less than** line 13, enter the difference	16	
17 Enter 10% of your adjusted gross income (Form 1040, line 33). Estates and trusts, see instructions	17	
18 Subtract line 17 from line 16. If zero or less, enter -0-. Also enter result on Schedule A (Form 1040), line 19. Estates and trusts, enter on the 'Other deductions' line of your tax return	18	

Name(s) Shown on Tax Return. Do Not Enter Name and Identifying Number if Shown on Page 1. | Identifying Number

Section B — Business and Income-Producing Property (Use this section to report casualties and thefts of property used in a trade or business or for income-producing purposes.)

Part I Casualty or Theft Gain or Loss (Use a separate Part I for each casualty or theft)

19 Description of properties (show type, location, and date acquired for each):

Property **A** ____________________

Property **B** ____________________

Property **C** ____________________

Property **D** ____________________

		Properties (Use a separate column for each property lost or damaged from one casualty or theft.)			
		A	**B**	**C**	**D**
20 Cost or adjusted basis of each property	20				
21 Insurance or other reimbursement (whether or not you filed a claim). See the instructions for line 3	21				
Note: *If ln 20 is* **more than** *ln 21, skip ln 22.* **22** Gain from casualty or theft. If line 21 is **more than** line 20, enter the difference here and on line 29 or line 34, column (c), except as provided in the instructions for line 33. Also, skip lines 23 through 27 for that column. See the instructions for line 4 if line 21 includes insurance or other reimbursement you did not claim, or you received payment for your loss in a later tax year	22				
23 Fair market value **before** casualty or theft	23				
24 Fair market value **after** casualty or theft	24				
25 Subtract line 24 from line 23	25				
26 Enter the **smaller** of line 20 or line 25 **Note:** *If the property was totally destroyed by casualty or lost from theft, enter on line 26 the amount from line 20.*	26				
27 Subtract ln 21 from ln 26. If zero or less, enter -0-	27				

28 Casualty or theft loss. Add the amounts on line 27. Enter the total here and on line 29 **or** line 34 (see instructions) . . . **28** ______

Part II Summary of Gains & Losses (from separate Parts I)

(a) Identify casualty or theft		**(b)** Losses from casualties or thefts: *(i)* Trade, business, rental or royalty property	*(ii)* Income-producing property	**(c)** Gains from casualties or thefts includible in income
Casualty or Theft of Property Held One Year or Less				
29				
30 Totals. Add the amounts on line 29	30			
31 Combine line 30, columns (b)(i) and (c). Enter the net gain or (loss) here and on Form 4797, line 14. If Form 4797 is not otherwise required, see instructions			31	
32 Enter the amount from line 30, column (b)(ii) here and on Schedule A (Form 1040), line 22. Partnerships, S corporations, estates and trusts, see instructions			32	
Casualty or Theft of Property Held More Than One Year				
33 Casualty or theft gains from Form 4797, line 32			33	
34				
35 Total losses. Add amounts on line 34, columns (b)(i) and (b)(ii)	35			
36 Total gains. Add lines 33 and 34, column (c)			36	
37 Add amounts on line 35, columns (b)(i) and (b)(ii)			37	
38 If the loss on line 37 is **more than** the gain on line 36:				
a Combine line 35, column (b)(i) and line 36, and enter the net gain or (loss) here. Partnerships and S corporations see the note below. All others enter this amount on Form 4797, line 14. If Form 4797 is not otherwise required, see instructions			38a	
b Enter the amount from line 35, column (b)(ii) here. Partnerships and S corporations see the note below. Individuals enter this amount on Schedule A (Form 1040), line 22. Estates and trusts, enter on the 'Other deductions' line of your tax return			38b	
39 If the loss on line 37 is **equal to** or **less than** the gain on line 36, combine these lines and enter here. Partnerships, see the note below. All others, enter this amount on Form 4797, line 3, column (g) and the net 28% rate gain or (loss), if applicable, in column (h)			39	

Note: *Partnerships, enter the amount from line 38a, 38b, or line 39 on Form 1065, Schedule K, line 7. S corporations, enter the amount from line 38a or 38b on Form 1120S, Schedule K, line 6.*

Form **4797**

Department of the Treasury
Internal Revenue Service (99)

Sales of Business Property

(Also Involuntary Conversions and Recapture Amounts Under Sections 179 and 280F(b)(2))

► **Attach to your tax return.** ► **See separate instructions.**

OMB No. 1545-0184

1997

27

Name(s) Shown on Return | Identifying Number

1 Enter here the gross proceeds from the sale or exchange of real estate reported to you for 1997 on Form(s) 1099-S (or a substitute statement) that you will be including on line 2, 10, or 20 1

Part I Sales or Exchanges of Property Used in a Trade or Business and Involuntary Conversions from Other Than Casualty or Theft – Property Held More Than 1 Year

2 (a) Description of property	(b) Date acquired (mo, day, yr)	(c) Date sold (mo, day, yr)	(d) Gross sales price	(e) Depreciation allowed or allowable since acquisition	(f) Cost or other basis, plus improvements and expense of sale	(g) Gain or (Loss) for entire year. Subtract (f) from the sum of (d) and (e)	(h) 28% Rate Gain or (Loss) * see instructions below

3 Gain, if any, from Form 4684, line 39	3		
4 Section 1231 gain from installment sales from Form 6252, line 26 or 37	4		
5 Section 1231 gain or (loss) from like-kind exchanges from Form 8824	5		
6 Gain, if any, from line 32, from other than casualty or theft	6		
7 Combine lines 2 through 6 in columns (g) and (h). Enter gain or (loss) here, and on the appropriate line as follows	7		

Partnerships – Enter the gain or (loss) on Form 1065, Schedule K, lines 6a and 6b. Skip lines 8, 9, 11, and 12 below.

S corporations – Report the gain or (loss) following the instructions for Form 1120S, Schedule K, lines 5 and 6. Skip lines 8, 9, 11, and 12 below, unless line 7, column (g) is a gain and the S corporation is subject to the capital gains tax.

All others – If line 7, column (g) is zero or a loss, enter that amount on line 11 below and skip lines 8 and 9. If line 7, column (g) is a gain and you did not have any prior year section 1231 losses, or they were recaptured in an earlier year, enter the gain or (loss) in each column as a long-term capital gain or (loss) on Schedule D and skip lines 8, 9, and 12 below.

8 Nonrecaptured net section 1231 losses from prior years (see instructions)	8		
9 Subtract line 8 from line 7. If zero or less, enter -0-. Also enter on the appropriate line as follows (see instructions)	9		

S corporations – Enter only the gain in column (g) on Schedule D (Form 1120S), line 14, and skip lines 11 and 12 below.

All others – If line 9, column (g) is zero, enter the gain from line 7, column (g) on line 12 below. If line 9, column (g) is more than zero, enter the amount from line 8, column (g) on line 12 below, and enter the gain or (loss) in each column of line 9 as a long-term capital gain or (loss) on Schedule D.

*Corporations (other than S corporations) should not complete column (h). Partnerships and S corporations must complete column (h). All others must complete column (h) only if line 7, column (g), is a gain. 28% rate gain or loss includes all gains and losses in column (g) from sales, exchanges, or conversions (including installment payments received) **either (a) before** 5/7/97 **or (b) after** 7/28/97 for assets held more than 1 year but not more than 18 months.

Part II Ordinary Gains and Losses

10 Ordinary gains and losses not included on lines 11 through 17 (include property held 1 year or less):

11 Loss, if any, from line 7, column (g)	11	
12 Gain, if any, from line 7, column (g) or amount from line 8, column (g) if applicable	12	
13 Gain, if any, from line 31	13	
14 Net gain or (loss) from Form 4684, lines 31 and 38a	14	
15 Ordinary gain from installment sales from Form 6252, line 25 or 36	15	
16 Ordinary gain or (loss) from like-kind exchanges from Form 8824	16	
17 Recapture of section 179 expense deduction for partners and S corporation shareholders from property dispositions by partnerships and S corporations (see instructions)	17	
18 Combine lines 10 through 17 in column (g). Enter gain or (loss) here, and on the appropriate line as follows	18	

a For all except individual returns: Enter the gain or (loss) from line 18 on the return being filed.

b For individual returns:

(1) If the loss on line 11 includes a loss from Form 4684, line 35, column (b)(ii), enter that part of the loss here and on line 22 of Schedule A (Form 1040). Identify as from 'Form 4797, line 18b(1).' (See instructions)	18b (1)	
(2) Redetermine the gain or (loss) on line 18, excluding the loss, if any, on line 18b(1). Enter here and on Form 1040, line 14	18b (2)	

Part III Gain from Disposition of Property Under Sections 1245, 1250, 1252, 1254, and 1255

19(a) Description of section 1245, 1250, 1252, 1254, or 1255 property:	**(b)** Date acquired (mo, day, yr)	**(c)** Date sold (mo, day, yr)
A		
B		
C		
D		

These columns relate to the properties on lines 19A through 19D ►		Property A	Property B	Property C	Property D
20 Gross sales price (**Note:** *See line 1 before completing.*)	**20**				
21 Cost or other basis plus expense of sale	**21**				
22 Depreciation (or depletion) allowed or allowable	**22**				
23 Adjusted basis. Subtract line 22 from line 21	**23**				
24 Total gain. Subtract line 23 from line 20	**24**				
25 If section 1245 property:					
a Depreciation allowed or allowable from line 22	**25a**				
b Enter the **smaller** of line 24 or 25a	**25b**				
26 If section 1250 property: If straight line depreciation was used, enter -0- on line 26g, except for a corporation subject to section 291.					
a Additional depreciation after 1975 (see instrs)	**26a**				
b Applicable percentage multiplied by the **smaller** of line 24 or line 26a	**26b**				
c Subtract line 26a from line 24. If residential rental property or line 24 is not more than line 26a, skip lines 26d and 26e	**26c**				
d Addn'l depreciation after 1969 and before 1976	**26d**				
e Enter the **smaller** of line 26c or 26d	**26e**				
f Section 291 amount (corporations only)	**26f**				
g Add lines 26b, 26e, and 26f	**26g**				
27 If section 1252 property: Skip this section if you did not dispose of farmland or if this form is being completed for a partnership.					
a Soil, water, and land clearing expenses	**27a**				
b Line 27a multiplied by applicable percentage	**27b**				
c Enter the **smaller** of line 24 or 27b	**27c**				
28 If section 1254 property:					
a Intangible drilling and development costs, expenditures for development of mines and other natural deposits, and mining exploration costs (see instrs)	**28a**				
b Enter the **smaller** of line 24 or 28a	**28b**				
29 If section 1255 property:					
a Applicable percentage of payments excluded from income under section 126 (see instructions)	**29a**				
b Enter the **smaller** of line 24 or 29a (see instrs)	**29b**				

Summary of Part III Gains. Complete property columns A through D through line 29b before going to line 30.

30 Total gains for all properties. Add property columns A through D, line 24	**30**	
31 Add property columns A through D, lines 25b, 26g, 27c, 28b, and 29b. Enter here and on line 13	**31**	
32 Subtract line 31 from line 30. Enter the portion from casualty or theft on Form 4684, line 33. Enter the portion from other than casualty or theft on Form 4797, line 6, column (g), and if applicable, column (h)	**32**	

Part IV Recapture Amounts Under Sections 179 and 280F(b)(2) When Business Use Drops to 50% or Less

See instructions.

		(a) Section 179	(b) Section 280F(b)(2)
33 Section 179 expense deduction or depreciation allowable in prior years	**33**		
34 Recomputed depreciation	**34**		
35 Recapture amount. Subtract line 34 from line 33. See instructions for where to report	**35**		

Form **8824**

Department of the Treasury
Internal Revenue Service

Like-Kind Exchanges

(and nonrecognition of gain from conflict-of-interest sales)

► **See separate instructions.** ► **Attach to your tax return.**
► **Use a separate form for each like-kind exchange.**

OMB No. 1545-1190

1997

49

Name(s) Shown on Tax Return | **Identifying Number**

Part I Information on the Like-Kind Exchange

Note: *If the property described on line 1 or line 2 is real or personal property located outside the United States, indicate the country.*

1 Description of like-kind property given up ► ______________________

2 Description of like-kind property received ► ______________________

3 Date like-kind property given up was originally acquired (month, day, year) 3

4 Date you actually transferred your property to other party (month, day, year) 4

5 Date the like-kind property you received was identified (month, day, year). See instructions 5

6 Date you actually received the like-kind property from other party (month, day, year) 6

7 Was the exchange made with a related party? If 'Yes', complete Part II. If 'No', go to Part III. See instructions.

a ☐ Yes, in this tax year **b** ☐ Yes, in a prior tax year **c** ☐ No

Part II Related Party Exchange Information

8 Name of Related Party | Related Party's Identifying Number

Address (number, street, and apartment, room, or suite number)

City or Town | State | ZIP Code | Relationship to You

9 During this tax year (and before the date that is 2 years after the last transfer of property that was part of the exchange), did the related party sell or dispose of the like-kind property received from you in the exchange? . . . . ☐ **Yes** ☐ **No**

10 During this tax year (and before the date that is 2 years after the last transfer of property that was part of the exchange), did you sell or dispose of the like-kind property you received? . . . . ☐ **Yes** ☐ **No**

If both lines 9 and 10 are 'No' and this is the year of the exchange, go to Part III. If either line 9 or line 10 is 'Yes,' the deferred gain or (loss) from line 24 **must** *be reported on your return this tax year,* **unless** *one of the exceptions on line 11 applies. See* **Related Party Exchanges** *in the instructions.*

11 If one of the exceptions below applies to the disposition, check the applicable box:

a ☐ The disposition was after the death of either of the related parties.

b ☐ The disposition was an involuntary conversion, and the threat of conversion occurred after the exchange.

c ☐ You can establish to the satisfaction of the IRS that neither the exchange nor the disposition had tax avoidance as its principal purpose. If this box is checked, attach an explanation. See instructions.

Part III Realized Gain or (Loss), Recognized Gain, and Basis of Like-Kind Property Received

Caution: *If you transferred* **and** *received* **(a)** *more than one group of like-kind properties, or* **(b)** *cash or other (not like-kind) property, see* **Reporting of multi-asset exchanges** *in the instructions.*

Note: *Complete lines 12 through 14* **only** *if you gave up property that was not like-kind. Otherwise, go to line 15.*

12 Fair market value (FMV) of other property given up 12

13 Adjusted basis of other property given up 13

14 Gain or (loss) recognized on other property given up. Subtract line 13 from line 12. Report the gain or (loss) in the same manner as if the exchange had been a sale 14

15 Cash received, FMV of other property received, plus net liabilities assumed by other party, reduced (but not below zero) by any exchange expenses you incurred. See instructions 15

16 FMV of like-kind property you received 16

17 Add lines 15 and 16 17

18 Adjusted basis of like-kind property you gave up, net amounts paid to other party, plus any exchange expenses **not** used on line 15. See instructions 18

19 **Realized gain or (loss).** Subtract line 18 from line 17 19

20 Enter the smaller of line 15 or line 19, but not less than zero 20

21 Ordinary income under recapture rules. Enter here and on Form 4797, line 16. See instructions 21

22 Subtract line 21 from line 20. If zero or less, enter -0-. If more than zero, enter here and on Schedule D or Form 4797, unless the installment method applies. See instructions 22

23 **Recognized gain.** Add lines 21 and 22 23

24 Deferred gain or (loss). Subtract line 23 from line 19. If a related party exchange, see instructions 24

25 **Basis of like-kind property received.** Subtract line 15 from the sum of lines 18 and 23 25

Name(s) Shown on Tax Return. Do Not Enter Name and Social Security Number if Shown on Page 1. | **Your Social Security Number**

Part IV **Section 1043 Conflict-of-Interest Sales** See instructions. Attach a copy of your certificate of divestiture.

Note: *This part is only to be used by officers or employees of the executive branch of the federal government for reporting nonrecognition of gain under section 1043 on the sale of property to comply with the conflict-of-interest requirements. This part can be used only if the cost of the replacement property exceeds the basis of the divested property.*

26 Description of divested property ► ______________________

27 Description of replacement prop. ► ______________________

28	Date divested property was sold (month, day, year)		28
29	Sales price of divested property. See instructions	29	
30	Basis of divested property	30	
31	**Realized gain.** Subtract line 30 from line 29		31
32	Cost of replacement property purchased within 60 days after date of sale	32	
33	Subtract line 32 from line 29. If zero or less, enter -0-		33
34	Ordinary income under recapture rules. Enter here and on Form 4797, line 10. See instructions		34
35	Subtract line 34 from line 33. If zero or less, enter -0-. If more than zero, enter here and on Schedule D or Form 4797. See instructions		35
36	**Recognized gain.** Add lines 34 and 35		36
37	Deferred gain. Subtract line 36 from line 31		37
38	**Basis of replacement property.** Subtract line 37 from line 32		38

Form **2106**

Department of the Treasury
Internal Revenue Service (99)

Employee Business Expense

► **See instructions.**
► **Attach to Form 1040.**

OMB No. 1545-0139

1997

54

Your Name	Social Security Number	Occupation in Which You Incurred Expenses

Part I Employee Business Expenses and Reimbursements

Step 1 Enter Your Expenses

		Column A Other than Meals and Entertainment	Column B Meals and Entertainment
1 Vehicle expense from line 22 or line 29	1		
2 Parking fees, tolls, and transportation, including train, bus, etc, that **did not** involve overnight travel or commuting to and from work	2		
3 Travel expense while away from home overnight, including lodging, airplane, car rental, etc. **Do not** include meals and entertainment	3		
4 Business expenses not included on lines 1 through 3. **Do not** include meals and entertainment	4		
5 Meals and entertainment expenses (see instructions)	5		
6 **Total expenses.** In column A, add lines 1 through 4 and enter the result. In column B, enter the amount from line 5	6		

Note: *If you were not reimbursed for any expenses in Step 1, skip line 7 and enter the amount from line 6 on line 8.*

Step 2 Enter Reimbursements Received from Your Employer for Expenses Listed in Step 1

7 Enter reimbursements received from your employer that were **not** reported to you in box 1 of Form W-2. Include any reimbursements reported under code 'L' in box 13 of your Form W-2 (see instructions)	7		

Step 3 Figure Expenses to Deduct on Schedule A (Form 1040)

8 Subtract line 7 from line 6	8		
Note: *If **both columns** of line 8 are zero, **stop here.** If column A is less than zero, report the amount as income on Form 1040, line 7.*			
9 In column A, enter the amount from line 8. In column B, multiply the amount on line 8 by 50% (.50). If either column is zero or less, enter -0- in that column	9		
10 Add the amounts on line 9 of both columns and enter the total here. **Also, enter the total on Schedule A (Form 1040), line 20.** (Fee-basis state or local government officials, qualified performing artists, and individuals with disabilities: See the instructions for special rules on where to enter the total.) ►		10	

BAA For Paperwork Reduction Act Notice, see separate instructions.

FDIA2712 10/21/97

Part II Vehicle Expenses (See instructions to find out which sections to complete.)

Section A – General Information

			(a) Vehicle 1	(b) Vehicle 2
11	Enter the date vehicle was placed in service	11		
12	Total miles vehicle was used during 1997	12	miles	miles
13	Business miles included on line 12	13	miles	miles
14	Percent of business use. Divide line 13 by line 12	14	%	%
15	Average daily round trip commuting distance	15	miles	miles
16	Commuting miles included on line 12	16	miles	miles
17	Other miles. Add lines 13 and 16 and subtract the total from line 12	17	miles	miles

18 Do you (or your spouse) have another vehicle available for personal purposes? ☐ Yes ☐ No

19 If your employer provided you with a vehicle, is personal use during off-duty hours permitted? ☐ Yes ☐ No ☐ Not applicable

20 Do you have evidence to support your deduction? ☐ Yes ☐ No

21 If 'Yes,' is the evidence written? ☐ Yes ☐ No

Section B – Standard Mileage Rate (Use this section only if you own the vehicle.)

22	Multiply line 13 by 31-1/2 ¢ (.315). Enter the result here and on line 1. (Rural mail carriers, see instructions)	22	

Section C – Actual Expenses

			(a) Vehicle 1		(b) Vehicle 2	
23	Gasoline, oil, repairs, vehicle insurance, etc	23				
24a	Vehicle rentals	24a				
b	Inclusion amount (see instructions)	24b				
c	Subtract line 24b from line 24a	24c				
25	Value of employer-provided vehicle (applies only if 100% of annual lease value was included on Form W-2 – see instructions)	25				
26	Add lines 23, 24c, and 25	26				
27	Multiply line 26 by the percentage on line 14	27				
28	Depreciation. Enter amount from line 38 below	28				
29	Add lines 27 and 28. Enter total here and on line 1	29				

Section D – Depreciation of Vehicles (Use this section only if you own the vehicle.)

			(a) Vehicle 1		(b) Vehicle 2	
30	Enter cost or other basis (see instructions)	30				
31	Enter amount of section 179 deduction (see instructions)	31				
32	Multiply line 30 by line 14 (see instructions if you elected the section 179 deduction)	32				
33	Enter depreciation method and percentage (see instructions)	33				
34	Multiply line 32 by the percentage on line 33 (see instructions)	34				
35	Add lines 31 and 34	35				
36	Enter the limit from the table in the line 36 instructions	36				
37	Multiply line 36 by the percentage on line 14	37				
38	Enter the **smaller** of line 35 or line 37. Also, enter this amount on line 28 above	38				

Form **2106-EZ**

Department of the Treasury
Internal Revenue Service (99)

Unreimbursed Employee Business Expenses

► **Attach to Form 1040.**

OMB No. 1545-1441

1997

54A

Your Name	**Social Security Number**	Occupation in Which You Incurred Expenses

Part I General Information

You may use this form Only if all of the following apply:

- You are an employee deducting expenses attributable to your job.
- You **do not** get reimbursed by your employer for any expenses (amounts your employer included in box 1 of your Form W-2 are not considered reimbursements).
- If you are claiming vehicle expense,

  a You own your own vehicle, and

  b You are using the standard mileage rate for 1997 **and** also used it for the year you first placed the vehicle in service.

Part II Figure Your Expenses

1	Vehicle expense using the standard mileage rate. Complete Part III and multiply line 8a by 31-1/2¢ (.315)	1	
2	Parking fees, tolls, and transportation, including train, bus, etc, that **did not** involve overnight travel or commuting to and from work	2	
3	Travel expense while away from home overnight, including lodging, airplane, car rental, etc. **Do not** include meals and entertainment	3	
4	Business expenses not included on lines 1 through 3. **Do not** include meals and entertainment	4	
5	Meals and entertainment expenses: $ ________ x 50% (.50)	5	
6	**Total expenses.** Add lines 1 through 5. Enter here and **on line 20 of Schedule A (Form 1040).** (Fee-basis state or local government officials, qualified performing artists, and individuals with disabilities: See instructions for special rules on where to enter this amount.)	6	

Part III Information on Your Vehicle.

Complete this part **Only** if you are claiming vehicle expense on line 1.

7 When did you place your vehicle in service for business purposes? (month, day, year) ► ________

8 Of the total number of miles you drove your vehicle during 1997, enter the number of miles you used your vehicle for:

a Business ________ **b** Commuting ________ **c** Other ________

9 Do you (or your spouse) have another vehicle available for personal use? ☐ **Yes** ☐ **No**

10 Was your vehicle available for use during off-duty hours? ☐ **Yes** ☐ **No**

11 **a** Do you have evidence to support your deduction? ☐ **Yes** ☐ **No**

b If 'Yes,' is the evidence written? ☐ **Yes** ☐ **No**

BAA For Paperwork Reduction Act Notice, see separate instructions.

Form **3903**

Department of the Treasury
Internal Revenue Service

Moving Expenses

► **Attach to Form 1040.**

OMB No. 1545-0062

1997

62

Name(s) Shown on Form 1040	**Your Social Security Number**

Caution: *If you are a member of the armed forces, see the instructions before completing this form.*

1 Enter the number of miles from your **old home** to your **new workplace**	1	**miles**	
2 Enter the number of miles from your **old home** to your **old workplace**	2	**miles**	
3 Subtract line 2 from line 1. Enter the result but not less than zero	3	**miles**	

Is line 3 at least 50 miles?

Yes. Go to line 4. Also, see **Time Test** in the instructions.

No. You **cannot** deduct your moving expenses. Do not complete the rest of this form.

4 Transportation and storage of household goods and personal effects (see instructions)	4	
5 Travel and lodging expenses of moving from your old home to your new home. **Do not** include meals (see instructions)	5	
6 Add lines 4 and 5	6	
7 Enter the total amount your employer paid for your move (including the value of services furnished in kind) that is **not** included in the wages box (box 1) of your W-2 form. This amount should be identified with code **P** in box 13 of your W-2 form	7	

Is line 6 more than line 7?

Yes. Go to line 8.

No. You **cannot** deduct your moving expenses. If line 6 is less than line 7, subtract line 6 from line 7 and include the result in income on Form 1040, line 7.

8 Subtract line 7 from line 6. Enter the result here and on Form 1040, line 25. This is your **moving expense deduction**	8	

BAA For Paperwork Reduction Act Notice, see separate instructions.

FDIA3701 10/17/97

Form **4562**

Department of the Treasury
Internal Revenue Service (99)

Depreciation and Amortization
(Including Information on Listed Property)

► See instructions.
► Attach this form to your return.

OMB No. 1545-0172

1997

67

Name(s) Shown on Return | Business or Activity to Which This Form Relates: Section 179 Summary | **Identifying Number**

Part I Election to Expense Certain Tangible Property (Section 179)
(Note: *If you have any 'listed property,' complete Part V before you complete Part I.)*

1	Maximum dollar limitation. If an enterprise zone business, see instructions	1	$18,000.
2	Total cost of section 179 property placed in service. See instructions	2	
3	Threshold cost of section 179 property before reduction in limitation	3	$200,000.
4	Reduction in limitation. Subtract line 3 from line 2. If zero or less, enter -0-	4	
5	Dollar limitation for tax year. Subtract line 4 from line 1. If zero or less, enter -0-. If married filing separately, see instructions	5	

6	(a) Description of property	(b) Cost (business use only)	(c) Elected cost
7	Listed property. Enter amount from line 27	7	

8	Total elected cost of section 179 property. Add amounts in column (c), lines 6 and 7	8	
9	Tentative deduction. Enter the smaller of line 5 or line 8	9	
10	Carryover of disallowed deduction from 1996. See instructions	10	
11	Business income limitation. Enter the smaller of business income (not less than zero) or line 5 (see instrs)	11	
12	Section 179 expense deduction. Add lines 9 and 10, but do not enter more than line 11	12	
13	Carryover of disallowed deduction to 1998. Add lines 9 and 10, less line 12 ►	13	

Note: *Do not use Part II or Part III below for listed property (automobiles, certain other vehicles, cellular telephones, certain computers, or property used for entertainment, recreation, or amusement). Instead, use Part V for listed property.*

Part II MACRS Depreciation for Assets Placed in Service Only During Your 1997 Tax Year
(Do Not Include Listed Property)

Section A – General Asset Account Election

14 If you are making the election under section 168(i)(4) to group any assets placed in service during the tax year into one or more general asset accounts, check this box. See instructions ► ☐

Section B – General Depreciation System (GDS) (See instructions)

(a) Classification of property	(b) Month and year placed in service	(c) Basis for depreciation (business/investment use only – see instructions)	(d) Recovery period	(e) Convention	(f) Method	(g) Depreciation deduction
15a 3-year property						
b 5-year property						
c 7-year property						
d 10-year property						
e 15-year property						
f 20-year property						
g 25-year property			25 yrs		S/L	
h Residential rental property			27.5 yrs	MM	S/L	
			27.5 yrs	MM	S/L	
i Nonresidential real property			39 yrs	MM	S/L	
				MM	S/L	

Section C – Alternative Depreciation System (ADS) (See instructions)

16a Class life					S/L	
b 12-year			12 yrs		S/L	
c 40-year			40 yrs	MM	S/L	

Part III Other Depreciation (Do Not Include Listed Property) (See instructions)

17	GDS and ADS deductions for assets placed in service in tax years beginning before 1997	17	
18	Property subject to section 168(f)(1) election	18	
19	ACRS and other depreciation	19	

Part IV Summary (See instructions)

20	Listed property. Enter amount from line 26	20	
21	**Total**. Add deductions on line 12, lines 15 and 16 in column (g), and lines 17 through 20. Enter here and on the appropriate lines of your return. Partnerships and S corporations – see instructions	21	
22	For assets shown above and placed in service during the current year, enter the portion of the basis attributable to section 263A costs	22	

Part V Listed Property — Automobiles, Certain Other Vehicles, Cellular Telephones, Certain Computers, and Property Used for Entertainment, Recreation, or Amusement

Note: *For any vehicle for which you are using the standard mileage rate or deducting lease expense, complete* **only** *23a, 23b, columns (a) through (c) of Section A, all of Section B, and Section C if applicable.*

Section A — Depreciation and Other Information (Caution: *See instructions for limits for passenger automobiles.*)

23a Do you have evidence to support the business/investment use claimed? ☐ Yes ☐ No **23b** If 'Yes,' is the evidence written? ☐ Yes ☐ No

(a) Type of property (list vehicles first)	(b) Date placed in service	(c) Business/investment use percentage	(d) Cost or other basis	(e) Basis for depreciation (business/investment use only)	(f) Recovery period	(g) Method/Convention	(h) Depreciation deduction	(i) Elected section 179 cost
24 Property used more than 50% in a qualified business use (see instructions):								
25 Property used 50% or less in a qualified business use (see instructions):								

26 Add amounts in column (h). Enter the total here and on line 20, page 1 . . . **26**

27 Add amounts in column (i). Enter the total here and on line 7, page 1 . . . **27**

Section B — Information On Use of Vehicles

Complete this section for vehicles used by a sole proprietor, partner, or other 'more than 5% owner,' or related person.
If you provided vehicles to your employees, first answer the questions in Section C to see if you meet an exception to completing this section for those vehicles.

	(a) Vehicle 1		(b) Vehicle 2		(c) Vehicle 3		(d) Vehicle 4		(e) Vehicle 5		(f) Vehicle 6	
28 Total business/investment miles driven during the year (**Do not** include commuting miles)												
29 Total commuting miles driven during the year												
30 Total other personal (noncommuting) miles driven												
31 Total miles driven during the year. Add lines 28 through 30												
	Yes	No	Yes	No	Yes	No	Yes	No	Yes	No	Yes	No
32 Was the vehicle available for personal use during off-duty hours?												
33 Was the vehicle used primarily by a more than 5% owner or related person?												
34 Is another vehicle available for personal use?												

Section C — Questions for Employers Who Provide Vehicles for Use by Their Employees

Answer these questions to determine if you meet an exception to completing Section B for vehicles used by employees who **are not** *more than 5% owners or related persons.*

	Yes	No
35 Do you maintain a written policy statement that prohibits all personal use of vehicles, including commuting, by your employees?		
36 Do you maintain a written policy statement that prohibits personal use of vehicles, except commuting, by your employees? See instructions for vehicles used by corporate officers, directors, or 1% or more owners		
37 Do you treat all use of vehicles by employees as personal use?		
38 Do you provide more than five vehicles to your employees, obtain information from your employees about the use of the vehicles, and retain the information received?		
39 Do you meet the requirements concerning qualified automobile demonstration use? See instructions		

Note: *If your answer to 35, 36, 37, 38, or 39 is 'Yes,' you need not complete Section B for the covered vehicles.*

Part VI Amortization

(a) Description of costs	(b) Date amortization begins	(c) Amortizable amount	(d) Code Section	(e) Amortization period or percentage	(f) Amortization for this year
40 Amortization of costs that begins during your 1997 tax year:					

41 Amortization of costs that began before 1997 . . . **41**

42 **Total.** Enter here and on 'Other Deductions' or 'Other Expenses' line of your return . . . **42**

SELECTED TAX RATE SCHEDULES
INSTRUCTIONS
AND OTHER INFORMATION

1997 Tax Rate Schedules

Caution: *Use **only** if your taxable income (Form 1040, line 38) is $100,000 or more. If less, use the **Tax Table.** Even though you cannot use the Tax Rate Schedules below if your taxable income is less than $100,000, all levels of taxable income are shown so taxpayers can see the tax rate that applies to each level.*

Schedule X—Use if your filing status is **Single**

If the amount on Form 1040, line 38, is: *Over—*	*But not over—*	Enter on Form 1040, line 39		*of the amount over—*
$0	$24,650	....	**15%**	**$0**
24,650	59,750	**$3,697.50 +**	**28%**	**24,650**
59,750	124,650	**13,525.50 +**	**31%**	**59,750**
124,650	271,050	**33,644.50 +**	**36%**	**124,650**
271,050	....	**86,348.50 +**	**39.6%**	**271,050**

Schedule Y-1—Use if your filing status is **Married filing jointly** or **Qualifying widow(er)**

If the amount on Form 1040, line 38, is: *Over—*	*But not over—*	Enter on Form 1040, line 39		*of the amount over—*
$0	$41,200	....	**15%**	**$0**
41,200	99,600	**$6,180.00 +**	**28%**	**41,200**
99,600	151,750	**22,532.00 +**	**31%**	**99,600**
151,750	271,050	**38,698.50 +**	**36%**	**151,750**
271,050	....	**81,646.50 +**	**39.6%**	**271,050**

Schedule Y-2—Use if your filing status is **Married filing separately**

If the amount on Form 1040, line 38, is: *Over—*	*But not over—*	Enter on Form 1040, line 39		*of the amount over—*
$0	$20,600	....	**15%**	**$0**
20,600	49,800	**$3,090.00 +**	**28%**	**20,600**
49,800	75,875	**11,266.00 +**	**31%**	**49,800**
75,875	135,525	**19,349.25 +**	**36%**	**75,875**
135,525	....	**40,823.25 +**	**39.6%**	**135,525**

Schedule Z—Use if your filing status is **Head of household**

If the amount on Form 1040, line 38, is: *Over—*	*But not over—*	Enter on Form 1040, line 39		*of the amount over—*
$0	$33,050	....	**15%**	**$0**
33,050	85,350	**$4,957.50 +**	**28%**	**33,050**
85,350	138,200	**19,601.50 +**	**31%**	**85,350**
138,200	271,050	**35,985.00 +**	**36%**	**138,200**
271,050	....	**83,811.00 +**	**39.6%**	**271,050**

expenses to deduct, report the amount shown in box 1 of your W-2 form on **Schedule C** or **C-EZ** along with your expenses.

Missing or Incorrect Form W-2?

If you do not get a W-2 form from your employer by February 2, 1998, use Tele-Tax topic 154 (see page 34) to find out what to do. Even if you do not get a W-2, you must still report your earnings on line 7. If you lose your Form W-2 or it is incorrect, ask your employer for a new one.

Line 8a

Taxable Interest

Each payer should send you a **Form 1099-INT** or **Form 1099-OID.** Report **all** of your taxable interest income on line 8a. But you must fill in and attach **Schedule B** if the total is over $400 or any of the other conditions listed at the beginning of the Schedule B instructions (see page B-1) apply to you.

Interest credited in 1997 on deposits that you could not withdraw because of the bankruptcy or insolvency of the financial institution may not have to be included in your 1997 income. For details, see **Pub. 550.**

TIP *If you get a 1997 Form 1099-INT for U.S. savings bond interest that includes amounts you reported before 1997, see Pub. 550.*

Line 8b

Tax-Exempt Interest

If you received any tax-exempt interest income, such as from municipal bonds, report it on line 8b. Include any exempt-interest dividends from a mutual fund or other regulated investment company. **Do not** include interest earned on your IRA.

Line 9

Dividends

Each payer should send you a **Form 1099-DIV.** You must fill in and attach **Schedule B** if your total gross dividends are over $400 or you received, as a nominee, dividends that actually belong to someone else. If you do not have to fill in Schedule B, include on line 9 only ordinary dividends and any investment expenses.

Capital Gain Distributions

If you received capital gain distributions, report them on **Schedule D.** If you are filing Schedule B, also report the distributions on that schedule.

Nontaxable Distributions

Some distributions are nontaxable because they are a return of your cost. They will not be taxed until you recover your cost. You must reduce your cost (or other basis) by these distributions. After you get back all of your cost (or other basis), you must report these distributions as capital gains. For details, see **Pub. 550.**

TIP *Dividends on insurance policies are a partial return of the premiums you paid. **Do not** report them as dividends. Include them in income only if they exceed the total of all net premiums you paid for the contract.*

Line 10

Taxable Refunds, Credits, or Offsets of State and Local Income Taxes

TIP *None of your refund is taxable if, in the year you paid the tax, you **did not** itemize deductions.*

If you received a refund, credit, or offset of state or local income taxes in 1997, you may receive a **Form 1099-G.** If you chose to apply part or all of the refund to your 1997 estimated state or local income tax, the amount applied is treated as received in 1997. If the refund was for a tax you paid in 1996 and you itemized deductions for 1996, use the worksheet on this page to see if any of your refund is taxable.

Exceptions

See **Recoveries** in **Pub. 525** instead of using the worksheet if **any** of the following apply:

- You received a refund in 1997 that is for a tax year other than 1996.
- You received a refund other than an income tax refund, such as a real property tax refund, in 1997 of an amount deducted or credit claimed in an earlier year.
- Your 1996 taxable income was less than zero.
- You made your last payment of 1996 estimated state or local income tax in 1997.
- You owed alternative minimum tax in 1996.
- You could not deduct the full amount of credits you were entitled to in 1996 because the total credits exceeded the tax shown on your 1996 Form 1040, line 38.
- You could be claimed as a dependent by someone else in 1996.

Also, see **Tax Benefit Rule** in Pub. 525 instead of using the worksheet if **all three** of the following apply.

1. You had to use the Itemized Deductions Worksheet in the 1996 Schedule A instructions because your 1996 adjusted gross income was over $117,950 (over $58,975 if married filing separately).

2. You could not deduct all of the amount on line 1 of the 1996 Itemized Deductions Worksheet.

3. The amount on line 8 of that 1996 worksheet would be more than the amount on line 4 of that worksheet if the amount on line 4 were reduced by 80% of the refund you received in 1997.

State and Local Income Tax Refund Worksheet—Line 10
(keep for your records)

1. Enter the income tax refund from **Form(s) 1099-G** (or similar statement). But **do not** enter more than the amount on your 1996 Schedule A (Form 1040), line 5 . . . . **1.** ________
2. Enter your total allowable itemized deductions from your 1996 Schedule A (Form 1040), line 28 . . . . **2.** ________

   Note: *If the filing status on your 1996 Form 1040 was married filing separately and your spouse itemized deductions in 1996, skip lines 3, 4, and 5 and enter the amount from line 2 on line 6.*
3. Enter on line 3 the amount shown below for the filing status claimed on your **1996** Form 1040:
   - Single, enter $4,000
   - Married filing jointly or Qualifying widow(er), enter $6,700
   - Married filing separately, enter $3,350
   - Head of household, enter $5,900

   } **3.** ________
4. Did you fill in line 33a on your 1996 Form 1040?

   No. Enter -0-.

   Yes. Multiply $800 ($1,000 if your 1996 filing status was single or head of household) by the number on line 33a of your 1996 Form 1040 . . . . **4.** ________
5. Add lines 3 and 4 . . . . **5.** ________
6. Subtract line 5 from line 2. If zero or less, enter -0- . . . . . **6.** ________
7. **Taxable part of your refund.** Enter the **smaller** of line 1 or line 6 here and on Form 1040, line 10 . . . . **7.** ________

Need More Information or Forms? You can use a personal computer, fax, or phone to get what you need. See page 4.

Deduction for Exemptions Worksheet—Line 37
(keep for your records)

1. Is the amount on Form 1040, line 33, more than the amount shown on line 4 below for your filing status?
   No. Stop. Multiply $2,650 by the total number of exemptions claimed on Form 1040, line 6d, and enter the result on line 37.
   Yes. Go to line 2.
2. Multiply $2,650 by the total number of exemptions claimed on Form 1040, line 6d . . . . 2. ______
3. Enter the amount from Form 1040, line 33 . . 3. ______
4. Enter the amount shown below for your filing status:
   - Married filing separately, enter $90,900
   - Single, enter $121,200
   - Head of household, enter $151,500
   - Married filing jointly or Qualifying widow(er), enter $181,800

   } 4. ______
5. Subtract line 4 from line 3. If zero or less, **stop;** enter the amount from line 2 above on Form 1040, line 37 . . . . 5. ______
   Note: *If line 5 is more than $122,500 (more than $61,250 if married filing separately),* ***stop;*** *you* ***cannot*** *take a deduction for exemptions. Enter -0- on Form 1040, line 37.*
6. Divide line 5 by $2,500 ($1,250 if married filing separately). If the result is not a whole number, round it up to the next higher whole number (for example, round 0.0004 to 1) . . . . . . 6. ______
7. Multiply line 6 by 2% (.02) and enter the result as a decimal amount . . . . 7. ___.___
8. Multiply line 2 by line 7 . . . . 8. ______
9. **Deduction for exemptions.** Subtract line 8 from line 2. Enter the result here and on Form 1040, line 37 . . . . 9. ______

Line 39

Tax

Use one of the following methods to figure your tax. Also include in the total on line 39 any tax from **Form 4972** and **Form 8814.** Be sure to check the appropriate box.

Tax Table

If your taxable income is less than $100,000, you **must** use the Tax Table to find your tax unless you are required to use **Form 8615** or **Schedule D.** The Tax Table starts on page 39. Be sure you use the correct column.

Tax Rate Schedules

You must use the Tax Rate Schedules on page 51 to figure your tax if your taxable income is $100,000 or more unless you are required to use **Form 8615** or **Schedule D.**

Schedule D

If you had a net capital gain on Schedule D and the amount on Form 1040, line 38, is more than zero, use Part IV of Schedule D to figure your tax.

Form 8615

Form 8615 must generally be used to figure the tax for any child who was under age 14 on January 1, 1998, and who had more than $1,300 of investment income, such as taxable interest or dividends. But if neither of the child's parents was alive on December 31, 1997, do not use Form 8615 to figure the child's tax.

Credits

Line 40

Credit for Child and Dependent Care Expenses

You may be able to take this credit if you paid someone to care for your child **under age 13** or your dependent or spouse who could not care for himself or herself. For details, use TeleTax topic 602 (see page 34) or see **Form 2441.**

Line 41

Credit for the Elderly or the Disabled

You may be able to take this credit if by the end of 1997 **(1)** you were age 65 or older, or **(2)** you retired on **permanent and total disability** and you had taxable disability income. But you usually **cannot** take the credit if the amount on Form 1040, line 33, is $17,500 or more ($20,000 if married filing jointly and only one spouse is eligible for the credit; $25,000 if married filing jointly and both spouses are eligible; $12,500 if married filing separately). See **Schedule R.**

Line 42

Adoption Credit

You may be able to take this credit if you paid expenses in 1997 to adopt a child and the adoption was final in or before 1997. See **Form 8839** for details.

Line 43

Foreign Tax Credit

If you paid income tax to a foreign country, see **Form 1116** to find out if you can take this credit.

Line 44

Other Credits

Include in the total on line 44 any of the following credits and check the appropriate box. If box **d** is checked, also enter the form number. To find out if you can take the credit, see the form or publication indicated.

- Mortgage interest credit. If a state or local government gave you a mortgage credit certificate, see **Form 8396.**
- Credit for prior year minimum tax. If you paid alternative minimum tax in a prior year, see **Form 8801.**
- Qualified electric vehicle credit. If you placed a new electric vehicle in service in 1997, see **Form 8834.**
- General business credit. This credit consists of a number of credits that usually apply only to individuals who are partners, shareholders in an S corporation, self-employed, or who have rental property. See **Form 3800** or **Pub. 334.**
- Empowerment zone employment credit. See **Form 8844.**
- District of Columbia first-time homebuyer credit. See **Form 8859.**

1997

Department of the Treasury
Internal Revenue Service

Instructions for Form 2106

Employee Business Expenses

Section references are to the Internal Revenue Code.

General Instructions

Changes To Note

- The standard mileage rate has been increased to 31½ cents for each mile of business use in 1997.
- For tax years ending after August 5, 1997, certain Federal employees engaged in criminal investigations can deduct expenses for travel away from their tax home for periods of more than one year. See the line 3 instructions.
- For tax years beginning after 1986, a fee-basis state or local government official can deduct the expenses incurred for services performed in that job in figuring adjusted gross income, rather than as a miscellaneous itemized deduction subject to the 2% limit. See page 2 for more details. You should file **Form 1040X** to amend any prior year income tax return affected by this retroactive change. However, you generally must file Form 1040X within 3 years after the date you filed your original return or within 2 years after the date you paid the tax, whichever is later.
- For property placed in service after August 5, 1997, the limits on depreciation and the section 179 expense deduction that apply solely to passenger automobiles have been **(a)** eliminated for the cost of installed qualified clean-fuel vehicle property and **(b)** tripled for certain electric vehicles. See page 4 for more details.

Purpose of Form

Use Form 2106 if you are an employee deducting expenses for your job. See the chart at the bottom of this page to find out if you must file this form.

You may be able to file **Form 2106-EZ,** Unreimbursed Employee Business Expenses, provided you use the standard mileage rate (if claiming vehicle expense) and are not reimbursed by your employer for any expense. See Form 2106-EZ to find out if you qualify to file it.

Recordkeeping

You cannot deduct expenses for travel (including meals unless you used the standard meal allowance), entertainment, gifts, or use of a car or other listed property, unless you keep records to prove the time, place, business purpose, business relationship (for entertainment and gifts), and amounts of these expenses. Generally, you must also have receipts for all lodging expenses (regardless of the amount) and any other expense of $75 or more.

Additional Information

If you need more information about employee business expenses, you will find the following publications helpful:

- **Pub. 463,** Travel, Entertainment, Gift, and Car Expenses
- **Pub. 529,** Miscellaneous Deductions
- **Pub. 587,** Business Use of Your Home (Including Use by Day-Care Providers)
- **Pub. 946,** How To Depreciate Property

Specific Instructions

Part I—Employee Business Expenses and Reimbursements

Fill in **all** of Part I if you were reimbursed for employee business expenses. If you were not reimbursed for your expenses, skip line 7 and complete the rest of Part I.

Step 1—Enter Your Expenses

Line 2. See the line 15 instructions for the definition of commuting.

Line 3. Enter expenses for lodging and transportation connected with overnight travel away from your tax home (defined later). **Do not** include expenses for meals and entertainment. For more details, including limits, see Pub. 463.

Who Must File Form 2106

- **A** Were you an employee during the year?
  - No → Do not file Form 2106. See the instructions for Schedule C, C-EZ, E, or F.
  - Yes → B
- **B** Did you have job-related business expenses?
  - No → Do not file Form 2106.
  - Yes → C
- **C** Were you reimbursed for any of your business expenses (count only reimbursements your employer **did not** include in box 1 of your Form W-2)?
  - No → D
  - Yes → F
- **D** Are you claiming job-related vehicle, travel, transportation, meals, or entertainment expenses?
  - Yes → File Form 2106 (but see **Notes** below).
  - No → E
- **E** Are you a fee-basis state or local government official, a qualified performing artist, or an individual with a disability claiming impairment-related work expenses? See the line 10 instructions for definitions.
  - Yes → File Form 2106 (but see **Notes** below).
  - No → Do not file Form 2106. Enter expenses on Schedule A (Form 1040), line 20. These expenses include business gifts, education (tuition and books), home office, trade publications, etc.
- **F** Did you use a vehicle in your job in 1997 that you also used for business in a prior year?
  - No → H
  - Yes → G
- **G** Is either **1** or **2** true?
  1. You used the actual expense method in the first year you used your vehicle for business.
  2. You used a depreciation method other than straight line for this vehicle in a prior year.
  - No → H
  - Yes → File Form 2106.
- **H** Are your deductible expenses more than your reimbursements (count only reimbursements your employer **did not** include in box 1 of your Form W-2)? For rules covering employer reporting of reimbursed expenses, see the instructions for line 7.
  - No → Do not file Form 2106.
  - Yes → File Form 2106 (but see **Notes** to the right).

Notes

- Generally, employee expenses are deductible only on line 20 of Schedule A (Form 1040). But **fee-basis state or local government officials, qualified performing artists,** and **individuals with disabilities** should see the instructions for line 10 to find out where to deduct employee expenses.
- Do not file Form 2106 if none of your expenses are deductible because of the 2% limit on miscellaneous itemized deductions.

Generally, you cannot deduct any expenses for travel away from your tax home for any period of temporary employment of more than 1 year. However, this rule does not apply for any period in which you were a Federal employee certified by the Attorney General as traveling in temporary duty status for the U.S. government to investigate a Federal crime (or to provide support services for the investigation of that crime).

Generally, your **tax home** is your main place of business or post of duty regardless of where you maintain your family home. If you do not have a regular or main place of business because of the nature of your work, then your tax home is the place where you regularly live. If you do not fit in either of these categories, you are considered an itinerant and your tax home is wherever you work. As an itinerant, you are not away from home and cannot claim a travel expense deduction. For more details on your tax home, see Pub. 463.

Line 4. Enter other job-related expenses not listed on any other line of this form. Include expenses for business gifts, education (tuition and books), home office, trade publications, etc. For details, including limits, see Pub. 463 and Pub. 529. If you are deducting home office expenses, see Pub. 587 for special instructions on how to report these expenses. If you are deducting depreciation or claiming a section 179 deduction on a cellular telephone or other similar telecommunications equipment, a home computer, etc., see **Form 4562,** Depreciation and Amortization, to figure the depreciation and section 179 deduction to enter on line 4.

Do not include expenses for meals and entertainment, taxes, or interest on line 4. Deductible taxes are entered on lines 5 through 9 of Schedule A (Form 1040). Employees cannot deduct car loan interest.

Note: *If line 4 is your only entry, do not complete Form 2106, unless you are:*

- *A fee-basis state or local government official claiming expenses in performing that job,*
- *A qualified performing artist claiming performing-arts-related business expenses,* ***or***
- *An individual with a disability claiming impairment-related work expenses.*

See the line 10 instructions for definitions. If you are not required to file Form 2106, enter your expenses directly on Schedule A (Form 1040), line 20.

Line 5. Enter your allowable meals and entertainment expense. Include meals while away from your tax home overnight and other business meals and entertainment. Instead of actual cost, you may be able to claim the **standard meal allowance** for your daily meals and incidental expenses while away from your tax home overnight. Under this method, you deduct a specified amount, depending on where you travel, instead of keeping records of your actual meal expenses. However, you must still keep records to prove the time, place, and business purpose of your travel. See Pub. 463 to figure your deduction using the standard meal allowance.

Step 2—Enter Reimbursements Received From Your Employer for Expenses Listed in STEP 1

Line 7. Enter reimbursements received from your employer (or third party) for expenses shown in Step 1 that were **not** reported to you in box 1 of your Form W-2. This includes reimbursements reported under code "L" in box 13 of Form W-2. Amounts reported under code "L" are certain reimbursements you received for business expenses that were not included as wages on Form W-2 because the expenses were treated as meeting specific IRS substantiation requirements.

Generally, when your employer pays for your expenses, the payments should not be included in box 1 of your Form W-2 if, within a reasonable period of time, you:

- Accounted to your employer for the expenses, **and**
- Were required to return, and did return, any payment not spent (or considered not spent) for business expenses.

If these payments were included in box 1, ask your employer for a corrected Form W-2.

Accounting to your employer means that you gave your employer documentary evidence and an account book, diary, or similar statement to verify the amount, time, place, and business purpose of each expense. You are also treated as having accounted for your expenses if either of the following applies:

- Your employer gave you a fixed travel allowance that is similar in form to the per diem allowance specified by the Federal Government and you verified the time, place, and business purpose of each expense.
- Your employer reimbursed you for vehicle expenses at the standard mileage rate or according to a flat rate or stated schedule, and you verified the date of each trip, mileage, and business purpose of the vehicle use.

See Pub. 463 for more details.

Allocating your reimbursement. If your employer paid you a single amount that covers meals and entertainment as well as other business expenses, you must allocate the reimbursement so that you know how much to enter in Column A and Column B of line 7. Use the following worksheet to figure this allocation.

Worksheet (keep for your records)

1.	Enter the total amount of reimbursements your employer gave you that **were not** reported to you in box 1 of Form W-2	______
2.	Enter the total amount of your expenses for the periods covered by this reimbursement	______
3.	Of the amount on line 2, enter your total expense for meals and entertainment	______
4.	Divide line 3 by line 2. Enter the result as a decimal (rounded to two places)	______
5.	Multiply line 1 by line 4. Enter the result here and in Column B, line 7..	______
6.	Subtract line 5 from line 1. Enter the result here and in Column A, line 7..	______

Step 3—Figure Expenses To Deduct on Schedule A (Form 1040)

Line 10—Special rules. If you were a **fee-basis state or local government official** (defined below), include the expenses you incurred for services performed in that job in the total on Form 1040, line 31. Write "FBO" and the amount in the space to the left of line 31 on Form 1040. Your employee business expenses are deductible whether or not you itemize deductions. A fee-basis state or local government official is an official who is an employee of a state or political subdivision of a state and is compensated, in whole or in part, on a fee basis.

If you were a **qualified performing artist** (defined below), include the part of the line 10 amount attributable to performing-arts-related expenses in the total on Form 1040, line 31. Write "QPA" and the amount in the space to the left of line 31 on Form 1040. Your performing-arts-related business expenses are deductible whether or not you itemize deductions.

A qualified performing artist is an individual who:

1. Performed services in the performing arts as an employee for at least two employers during the tax year,

2. Received from at least two of those employers wages of $200 or more per employer,

3. Had allowable business expenses attributable to the performing arts of more than 10% of gross income from the performing arts, **and**

4. Had adjusted gross income of $16,000 or less before deducting expenses as a performing artist.

To be treated as a qualified performing artist, a married individual must also file a joint return, unless the individual and his or her spouse lived apart for all of 1997. On a joint return, requirements **1, 2,** and **3** must be figured separately for each spouse. However, requirement **4** applies to the combined adjusted gross income of both spouses.

If you were an **individual with a disability** and are claiming impairment-related work expenses (defined below), enter the part of the line 10 amount attributable to those expenses on Schedule A, line 27, instead of on Schedule A, line 20. Your impairment-related work expenses are not subject to the 2% limit that applies to most other employee business expenses.

Impairment-related work expenses are the allowable expenses of an individual with physical or mental disabilities for attendant care at his or her place of employment. They also include other expenses in connection with the place of employment that enable the employee to work. See Pub. 463 for more details.

Part II—Vehicle Expenses

There are two methods for computing vehicle expenses—the Standard Mileage Rate and the Actual Expense Method. In some cases, you must use the Actual Expense Method instead of the Standard Mileage Rate. Use the following flowchart to see which method to use. Rural mail carriers should see the line 22 instructions for special rules that apply to them instead of using the flowchart.

If you have the option of using either the Standard Mileage Rate or Actual Expense Method, you should figure your expenses both ways to find the method most beneficial to you. But when completing Form 2106, fill in **only** the sections that apply to the method you choose.

For Vehicles Placed in Service After 1980*

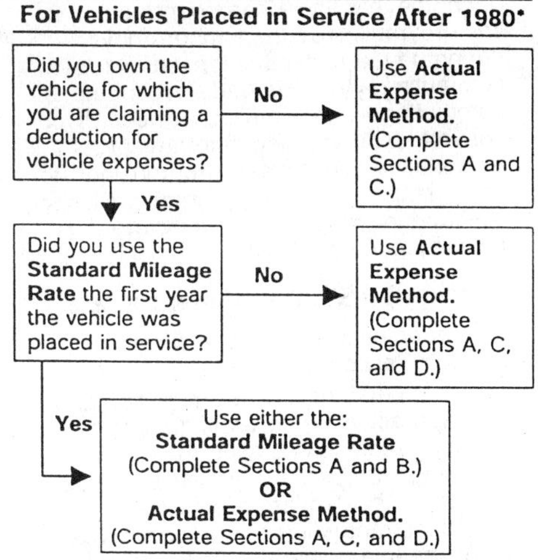

* For vehicles placed in service before 1981, see Rev. Proc. 96-63, 1996-2 C.B. 420.

Section A—General Information

All individuals claiming vehicle expenses must complete Section A.

If you used two vehicles for business during the year, use a separate column in Sections A, C, and D for each vehicle. If you used more than two vehicles, attach a statement using the format in Sections A, C, and D.

Line 11. Date placed in service is generally the date you first start using your vehicle. However, if you first start using your vehicle for personal use and later convert it to business use, the vehicle is treated as placed in service on the date you started using it for business.

Line 12. Enter the total miles you drove each vehicle during the year for all purposes. However, if you converted your vehicle during the year from personal to business use (or from business to personal use), enter the total miles for only the months you drove the vehicle for business purposes.

Line 13. Do not include commuting miles on this line; commuting miles are not considered business miles. See the line 15 instructions for the definition of **commuting.**

Line 14. Divide line 13 by line 12 to figure your business use percentage. However, if you converted your vehicle during the year from personal to business use (or from business to personal use), multiply this percentage by the number of months you drove the vehicle for business purposes and divide the result by 12.

Line 15. Enter your average daily round trip commuting distance. If you went to more than one work location, figure the average.

Generally, **commuting** is travel between your home and a work location. However, such travel is not commuting if you meet **any** of the following conditions:

- You have at least one regular work location away from your home and you travel to a temporary work location in the same trade or business, regardless of the distance. A temporary work location is one where you perform services on an irregular or short-term basis (generally a matter of days or weeks).
- You travel to a temporary work location outside the metropolitan area where you live and normally work.
- Your home is your principal place of business under section 280A(c)(1)(A) (for purposes of deducting expenses for business use of your home) and you travel to another work location in the same trade or business, regardless of whether that location is regular or temporary and regardless of distance.

Line 16. If you do not know the total actual miles you used your vehicle for commuting during the year, figure the amount to enter on line 16 by multiplying the number of days during the year that you used each vehicle for commuting by the average daily round trip commuting distance in miles. However, if you converted your vehicle during the year from personal to business use (or from business to personal use), enter your commuting miles only for the period you drove your vehicle for business purposes.

Section B—Standard Mileage Rate

If you do not own the vehicle, skip Section B and go to Section C.

You may use the standard mileage rate instead of actual expenses to figure the deductible costs of operating a passenger car, including a van, pickup, or panel truck. If you want to use the standard mileage rate, you must do so in the first year you place your car in service. In later years, you may deduct actual expenses but you may not use a depreciation method other than straight line. If you do not use the standard mileage rate in the first year, you may not use it for that car for any later year.

You may also deduct state and local personal property taxes. Enter these taxes on Schedule A (Form 1040), line 7.

Line 22. If you were a rural mail carrier (defined below) in 1997 and you use the standard mileage rate to figure your vehicle expense, multiply the number of miles on line 13 by **47¼ cents** (.4725) instead of 31½ cents.

You are considered a **rural mail carrier** only if you:

- Were an employee of the U.S. Postal Service,
- Used your own vehicle to collect and deliver mail on a rural route, and
- Did not claim depreciation for the vehicle for any tax year beginning after 1987.

If you are also claiming the standard mileage rate for mileage driven in another business activity, you must figure the deduction for that mileage on a separate Form 2106.

See Pub. 463 for more details.

Section C—Actual Expenses

Line 23. Enter your total annual expenses for gasoline, oil, repairs, insurance, tires, license plates, or similar items. Do not include state and local personal property taxes or interest expense you paid. Deduct state and local personal property taxes on Schedule A (Form 1040), line 7. Employees cannot deduct car loan interest.

Line 24a. If you rented or leased a vehicle during the year instead of using one you own, enter the cost of renting. Also, include on this line any temporary vehicle rentals not included on line 3, such as when your car was being repaired.

Line 24b. If you leased a vehicle for a term of 30 days or more after June 18, 1984, you may have to reduce your deduction for vehicle lease payments by an amount called the **inclusion amount.** You may have to enter the inclusion amount on line 24b if:

The lease term began in:	And the vehicle's fair market value on the first day of the lease exceeded:
1997	$15,800
1995 or 1996	$15,500
1994	$14,600
1993	$14,300

If the lease term began before 1993, see Pub. 463 to find out if you have an inclusion amount and how to figure the inclusion amount. Enter the inclusion amount on line 24b. If you have no inclusion amount, leave line 24b blank.

Line 25. If during 1997 your employer provided a vehicle for your business use and included 100% of its annual lease value in box 1 of your Form W-2, enter this amount on line 25. If less than 100% of the annual lease value was included in box 1 of your Form W-2, skip line 25.

Section D—Depreciation of Vehicles

Depreciation is an amount you can deduct to recover the cost or other basis of your vehicle over a certain number of years. In some cases, you may elect to expense, under section 179, part of the cost of your vehicle in the year of purchase. For more details, see Pub. 463.

Line 30. Enter the vehicle's actual cost (including sales tax) or other basis (unadjusted for prior years' depreciation). If you traded in your vehicle, your basis is the adjusted basis of the old vehicle (figured as if 100% of the vehicle's use had been for business purposes) plus any additional amount you pay for your new vehicle. Reduce your basis by any diesel fuel tax credit, qualified electric vehicle credit, or deduction for clean-fuel vehicles you claimed.

If you converted the vehicle from personal use to business use, your basis for depreciation is the smaller of the vehicle's adjusted basis or its fair market value on the date of conversion.

Line 31. If 1997 is the first year your vehicle was placed in service and the percentage on line 14 is more than 50%, you may elect to deduct as an expense a portion of the cost (subject to a yearly limit). To calculate this section 179 deduction, multiply the part of the cost of the vehicle that you choose to expense by the percentage on line 14. The total of your depreciation and section 179 deduction generally cannot be more than $3,160 multiplied by the percentage on line 14. However, the $3,160 limit is increased for certain clean-fuel and electric vehicles. See the footnote in the line 36 instructions for more details. Your section 179 deduction for the year cannot be more than the income from your job and any other active trade or business on your Form 1040.

Caution: *If you are claiming a section 179 deduction on other property, or you placed more than $200,000 of section 179 property in service during the year, use Form 4562 to figure your section 179 deduction. Enter the amount of the section 179 deduction allocable to your vehicle (from Form 4562, line 12) on Form 2106, line 31.*

Note: *For section 179 purposes, the cost of the new vehicle does not include the adjusted basis of the vehicle you traded in.*

Example:

Cost including taxes		$15,000
Adjusted basis of trade-in	−	$ 2,000
Section 179 basis	=	$13,000
Limit on depreciation and section 179 deduction		$ 3,160
Smaller of:		
Section 179 basis, or limit on depreciation and section 179 deduction		$ 3,160
Percentage on line 14	×	75%
Section 179 deduction	=	$ 2,370

Line 32. To figure the basis for depreciation, multiply line 30 by the percentage on line 14. From that result, subtract the full amount of any section 179 deduction (and half of any investment credit taken before 1986 unless you took the reduced credit).

Line 33. If you used the standard mileage rate in the first year the vehicle was placed in service and now elect to use the actual expense method, you **must** use the straight line method of depreciation for the vehicle's estimated useful life. Otherwise, use the chart on page 4 to find the depreciation method and percentage to enter on line 33. (For example, if you placed a car in service on December 1, 1997, and you use the method and percentage in column (a), enter "200DB5%" on line 33.) To use the chart, first find the date you placed the vehicle in service (line 11). Then, select the depreciation method and percentage from column (a), (b), (c), or (d). For vehicles placed in service before 1997, use the same method you used on last year's return unless a decline in your business use requires a change to the straight line method. For vehicles placed in service during 1997, select the depreciation method and percentage after reading the explanation for each column.

Depreciation Method and Percentage Chart				
Date Placed in Service	(a)	(b)	(c)	(d)
Oct. 1—Dec. 31, 1997	200 DB 5%	150 DB 3.75%	SL 2.5%	
Jan. 1—Sept. 30, 1997	200 DB 20%	150 DB 15%	SL 10%	
Oct. 1—Dec. 31, 1996	200 DB 38%	150 DB 28.88%	SL 20%	
Jan. 1—Sept. 30, 1996	200 DB 32%	150 DB 25.5%	SL 20%	
Oct. 1—Dec. 31, 1995	200 DB 22.8%	150 DB 20.21%	SL 20%	
Jan. 1—Sept. 30, 1995	200 DB 19.2%	150 DB 17.85%	SL 20%	
Oct. 1—Dec. 31, 1994	200 DB 13.68%	150 DB 16.4%	SL 20%	
Jan. 1—Sept. 30, 1994	200 DB 11.52%	150 DB 16.66%	SL 20%	
Oct. 1—Dec. 31, 1993	200 DB 10.94%	150 DB 16.41%	SL 20%	
Jan. 1—Sept. 30, 1993	200 DB 11.52%	150 DB 16.66%	SL 20%	
Oct. 1—Dec. 31, 1992	200 DB 9.58%	150 DB 14.35%	SL 17.5%	
Jan. 1—Sept. 30, 1992	200 DB 5.76%	150 DB 8.33%	SL 10%	
Jan. 1, 1987—Dec. 31, 1991	MACRS*	MACRS*	SL*	
Jan. 1—Dec. 31, 1986	ACRS*		SL*	SL 8.333%
Jan. 1—Dec. 31, 1985	ACRS*		SL*	SL 4.167%
June 19—Dec. 31, 1984	ACRS*		SL*	

*Enter your unrecovered basis, if any, on line 34. See Pub. 463 for more information.

Column (a). You may use column (a) only if the business use percentage on line 14 is more than 50%. The method in this column, the 200% declining balance method, will give you the largest deduction in the year your vehicle is placed in service. This column is also used for vehicles placed in service before 1987 and depreciated under the accelerated cost recovery system (ACRS).

Column (b). You may use column (b) only if the business use percentage on line 14 is more than 50%. The method in this column, the 150% declining balance method, will give you a smaller depreciation deduction than in column (a) for the first 3 years. However, you will not have a "depreciation adjustment" on this item for alternative minimum tax purposes. This may result in a smaller tax liability if you must file **Form 6251,** Alternative Minimum Tax—Individuals.

Column (c). You must use column (c), or column (d) if applicable, if the business use percentage on line 14 is 50% or less. The method in this column is the straight line method over 5 years. It is optional if the business use percentage on line 14 is more than 50%.

Note: *If your vehicle was used more than 50% for business in the year it was placed in service and used 50% or less in a later year, part of the depreciation and section 179 deduction previously claimed may have to be added back to your income in the later year. Figure the amount to be included in income on **Form 4797,** Sales of Business Property.*

Column (d). You must use column (d) if you placed your vehicle in service before 1987 and you elected the straight line method over a recovery period of 12 years.

Caution: *If you placed other business property in service during the year you placed your vehicle in service (for any year after 1986), or you used your vehicle mainly within an Indian reservation, you may not be able to use the chart. See Pub. 946 to figure your depreciation.*

Line 34. If during the year you did not sell or exchange your vehicle (or you sold or exchanged your vehicle that was placed in service after 1986 and before 1992), multiply line 32 by the percentage on line 33. If during the year you sold or exchanged your vehicle that was placed in service:

- Before 1987, enter -0- on line 34 for that vehicle.
- After 1991, multiply the result for line 34 by 50%, and enter on line 34. However, do not multiply by 50% if you originally placed the vehicle in service during the last 3 months of a year after 1991. Instead, multiply the result for line 34 by the percentage shown below for the month you disposed of the vehicle:

Month	Percentage
Jan., Feb., March	12.5%
April, May, June	37.5%
July, Aug., Sept.	62.5%
Oct., Nov., Dec.	87.5%

Line 36. Using the chart below, find the date you placed your vehicle in service. Then, enter on line 36 the corresponding amount from the **Limit** column.

Date Vehicle Was Placed in Service	Limit
Jan. 1—Dec. 31, 1997	$3,160*
Jan. 1—Dec. 31, 1996	$4,900
Jan. 1—Dec. 31, 1995	$2,950
Jan. 1, 1993—Dec. 31, 1994	$1,675
Jan. 1, 1991—Dec. 31, 1992	$1,575
Jan. 1, 1987—Dec. 31, 1990	$1,475
Apr. 3, 1985—Dec. 31, 1986	$4,800
Jan. 1—Apr. 2, 1985	$6,200
June 19—Dec. 31, 1984	$6,000

*For vehicles placed in service after August 5, 1997:
- This limit does not apply to the cost of any qualified clean-fuel vehicle property (such as retrofit parts and components) installed on a vehicle for the purpose of permitting that vehicle to run on a clean-burning fuel. See section 179A for definitions.
- The limit is $9,480 for vehicles produced by an original equipment manufacturer and designed to run primarily on electricity.

Paperwork Reduction Act Notice. We ask for the information on this form to carry out the Internal Revenue laws of the United States. You are required to give us the information. We need it to ensure that you are complying with these laws and to allow us to figure and collect the right amount of tax.

You are not required to provide the information requested on a form that is subject to the Paperwork Reduction Act unless the form displays a valid OMB control number. Books or records relating to a form or its instructions must be retained as long as their contents may become material in the administration of any Internal Revenue law. Generally, tax returns and return information are confidential, as required by section 6103.

The time needed to complete and file this form will vary depending on individual circumstances. The estimated average time is:

Recordkeeping	1 hr., 38 min.
Learning about the law or the form	20 min.
Preparing the form	1 hr., 13 min.
Copying, assembling, and sending the form to the IRS	41 min.

If you have comments concerning the accuracy of these time estimates or suggestions for making this form simpler, we would be happy to hear from you. See the Instructions for Form 1040.

1997

Department of the Treasury
Internal Revenue Service

Instructions for Form 2119

Sale of Your Home

General Instructions

Changes To Note

New rules for sales after May 6, 1997. If you sold your main home after May 6, 1997, you may be able to exclude up to $250,000 of the gain from the sale regardless of your age. If you are married filing a joint return, you may be able to exclude up to $500,000. Any gain in excess of your exclusion is taxable. You may be able to elect to use the rules that apply to sales before May 7, 1997. For more details, see **Sales After May 6, 1997** on page 3.

Basis adjustment for certain Form 8839 filers. You must reduce your basis by any credit or exclusion you are claiming on **Form 8839,** Qualified Adoption Expenses, for the cost of capital improvements to your home.

Purpose of Form

Use Form 2119 to report the sale of your main home. If you qualify, also use Form 2119 to:

- Claim the exclusion for sales after May 6, 1997, or
- Elect the one-time exclusion for people who were age 55 or older on the date of sale, or
- Postpone paying tax on all or part of the gain.

Caution: *If the home you sold was financed (in whole or in part) from a qualified mortgage credit certificate or the proceeds of a tax-exempt qualified mortgage bond, you may owe additional tax. See **Form 8828,** Recapture of Federal Mortgage Subsidy, for details.*

Who Must File

You must file Form 2119 for the year in which you sell your main home. You must do this even if the sale resulted in a loss or you can exclude or postpone all or part of the gain. You must also file Form 1040 if your gross income is at least equal to a certain amount. For details, see **Chart A** in the instructions for Form 1040. If you must file Form 1040, attach Form 2119 to your return. There may be other filing requirements as well. See **When and Where To File** on this page.

Loss on the sale of your home. You cannot deduct a loss on the sale of your home. However, you must file Form 2119 to report the sale. Complete lines 1 through 8 of Form 2119 for the year of sale. If you replace your home, the loss has no effect on the basis of your new home.

Additional Information

You may find **Pub. 523,** Selling Your Home, helpful. It has examples of how to complete Form 2119.

Definitions

Basis. If you bought your home, your basis is the purchase price of the home minus certain seller-paid points (see page 4). If you acquired your home other than by purchase, such as by gift, inheritance, or trade, or you built your home, see Pub. 523. For a complete discussion of basis, see **Pub. 551,** Basis of Assets.

Adjusted basis. This is your basis in the property increased or decreased by certain amounts. For details on how to figure the adjusted basis of the home you sold, see the instructions for line 7 on page 4.

Date of sale. See the instructions for line 1 on page 3.

Main home. Your main home is the one you live in most of the time. It can be a house, houseboat, house trailer, cooperative apartment, condominium, etc.

Replacement period. This is the time period during which you must replace your old main home to postpone any of the gain from its sale. It starts 2 years before and ends 2 years after the date of sale. But this period may be longer if you are on active duty in the U.S. Armed Forces for more than 90 days or if you live and work outside the United States. For details, see Pub. 523.

Special Situations

More than one owner. If you owned the old home jointly with a person other than your spouse, you may exclude or postpone gain only on your ownership interest in the home. For more details, see Pub. 523.

Surviving spouse. If your spouse died before the old home was sold and you owned the home jointly with your deceased spouse, you must make a special computation to figure the adjusted basis of the home you sold. For details, see **Home received as inheritance** under **Basis** in Pub. 523.

Divorced or separated taxpayers. If your home was sold in connection with a divorce or separation, see Pub. 523. Also, see **Pub. 504,** Divorced or Separated Individuals.

Condemned property. If your old home was condemned for public use, you can choose either to postpone gain under the rules for a condemnation or to treat the transaction as a sale of your home. See Pub. 523. Also, see **Pub. 544,** Sales and Other Dispositions of Assets.

Partial rental or business use of home. If part of your old home was rented out or used for business, you may have to report that part of the sale on **Form 4797,** Sales of Business Property. See the instructions for line 3 on page 3.

Installment sale. If you provided financing for the buyer of your home, you may be able to choose to report the gain on the sale using the installment method. For details, see **Pub. 537,** Installment Sales. If you qualify and choose to do so, complete Form 2119 first and then complete **Form 6252,** Installment Sale Income. Also, see the instructions for line 15 on page 4. **Do not** report the gain from Form 2119 on Schedule D (Form 1040).

Note: *Be sure to report on Form 1040, line 8a, any interest you received on the note or other financial instrument. If the buyer used the property as a personal residence, be sure you report that buyer's name, social security number, and address on Schedule B (Form 1040).*

Casualty damage. If your home was damaged by fire, storm, or other casualty, see **Form 4684,** Casualties and Thefts, and its separate instructions. Also, see **Pub. 547,** Casualties, Disasters, and Thefts (Business and Nonbusiness).

When and Where To File

File Form 2119 for the year of sale.

Note: *The additional filing requirements explained next do not apply to sales after May 6, 1997, unless you qualify for and elect to use the rules that apply to sales before May 7, 1997. They also do not apply if the amount on line 8 of Form 2119 is zero or less, even if you replace your home.*

Additional filing requirements. If you are using the rules that apply to sales before May 7, 1997, and you have not replaced your home but plan to do so within the replacement period (defined on this page), you will also have to complete a second Form 2119.

- You must file the second Form 2119 by itself if **all three** of the following apply:

1. You planned to replace your home within the replacement period.

(continued)

2. You later replaced your home within the replacement period.

3. Your taxable gain (line 21 on the second Form 2119) is zero.

If your taxable gain is zero, no tax is due. But you must still file the second form to show that you replaced your home within the replacement period. Enter your name and address, and sign and date the second form. If a joint return was filed for the year of sale, both you and your spouse must sign the second Form 2119. Send the form to the Internal Revenue Service Center for the place where you now live.

- You must file **Form 1040X,** Amended U.S. Individual Income Tax Return, for the year of sale with the second Form 2119 attached if **any** of the following apply:

1. You planned to replace your home when you filed your tax return, you later replaced your home within the replacement period, **and** you had a taxable gain on line 21 of the second Form 2119.

2. You planned to replace your home when you filed your tax return but **did not** do so within the replacement period.

3. You **did not** plan to replace your home when you filed your tax return and included the gain in income, but later you did replace your home within the replacement period.

Report the correct amount of gain from Form 2119 on Schedule D (Form 1040) and attach both forms to Form 1040X. Interest will be charged on any additional tax due. If you are due a refund, any interest will be included with the refund.

Recordkeeping

Keep a copy of Form 2119 (and any documents used to complete it) with your tax return for the year of sale until the statute of limitations runs out for that return. Usually, this is 3 years from the date the return was due or filed, or 2 years from the date the tax was paid, whichever is later. (See Pub. 523 for more details.) But if you postpone tax on any gain, keep a copy of the Form 2119 (and any documents used to complete it) with your records for the basis of your new home.

Sales Before May 7, 1997

If you sold your main home before May 7, 1997, you may be able to:

- Elect to take the one-time exclusion explained next for people age 55 or older, or
- Postpone all or part of the gain (see **Postponing Gain** on this page).

One-Time Exclusion for People Age 55 or Older

Generally, you can elect to exclude from your income up to $125,000 ($62,500 if married filing a separate return) of the gain from one sale of any main home you choose. The gain excluded is never taxed. But for sales after July 26, 1978, the exclusion is available only once. You can make the election if **all three** of the following apply:

1. You or your spouse were age 55 or older on the date of sale.

2. Neither you nor your spouse have ever excluded gain on the sale of a home after July 26, 1978.

3. The person who was age 55 or older owned and lived in the home for periods adding up to at least 3 years within the 5-year period ending on the date of sale. But see **Exception for temporary absences** and **Exception for individuals with a disability** on this page.

To make the election for this sale, complete Part II. If the gain is more than the amount excluded, also complete Part III to figure whether the excess gain is included in your income or postponed. If the gain is less than $125,000 ($62,500 if married filing a separate return), the difference **cannot** be excluded on a future sale of another main home. Generally, you can make or revoke the election within 3 years from the due date of your return (including extensions) for the year of sale. To do so, file Form 1040X with Form 2119 attached. For more details, see Pub. 523.

Exception for temporary absences. You can count short temporary absences such as for vacations or other seasonal absences as time lived in the home even if you rented the home during the absences.

Exception for individuals with a disability. If you meet this exception, you are treated as having lived in the home sold during any time that you lived in a facility such as a nursing home. The facility must be licensed by a state or political subdivision to care for people with your condition. You meet this exception if, during the 5-year period ending on the date of sale—

- You became physically or mentally unable to care for yourself, and
- You owned and lived in your home as your main home for a total of at least 1 year.

Previous home destroyed or condemned. You may be able to count time you owned and lived in a previous home that was destroyed or condemned. For details, see Pub. 523.

Married persons. If you and your spouse owned the property jointly and file a joint return, only one of you must meet the age, ownership, and use tests to be able to make the election. If you did not own the property jointly, the spouse who owned the property must meet these tests.

If you were married at the time of sale, both you and your spouse must agree to exclude the gain. If you do not file a joint return with that spouse, your spouse must agree to exclude the gain by signing a statement saying, "I agree to the Part II election." The statement and signature may be made on a separate sheet or in the bottom margin on page 1 of Form 2119.

If you sell a home while you are married and one spouse already made the election prior to the marriage, neither of you can exclude gain on the sale.

The election to exclude gain applies to both you and your spouse. If you elect to exclude gain during marriage and later divorce, neither of you can make the election again.

Postponing Gain

If you buy or build another main home and move into it within the replacement period (defined on page 1), you must postpone all or part of the gain in most cases. The amount of gain postponed is shown on line 22.

If one spouse dies after the old home is sold and before the new home is bought, the gain from the sale of the old home is postponed if **(1)** the above requirements are met, **(2)** the spouses were married on the date of death, and **(3)** the surviving spouse uses the new home as his or her main home. This rule applies whether the title of the old home is in one spouse's name or is held jointly. For more details, see **Deceased spouse** in Pub. 523.

If you bought more than one main home during the replacement period, only the last one you bought qualifies as your new main home for postponing gain. If you sold more than one main home during the replacement period, any sale after the first one does not qualify for postponing gain. But these rules do not apply if you sold your home because of a job change and you meet the time and distance requirements explained in **Pub. 521,** Moving Expenses. If this is the case, file a Form 2119 for each sale, for the year of the sale, and attach an explanation for each sale (except the first) to Form 2119.

Dividing the gain between you and your spouse. If you are married and you or your spouse owned the old home separately but own the new home jointly, you and your spouse may elect to divide the gain and the adjusted basis. If you owned the old home jointly but you now own new homes separately, you may elect to divide the gain to be postponed. In either situation, you both must:

1. Use the old and new homes as your main homes, and

2. Sign a statement that says, "We agree to reduce the basis of the new home(s) by the gain from selling the old home." This statement can be made in the bottom margin on page 1 of Form 2119 or on an attached sheet.

If you both do not meet these two requirements, you must report the gain in the regular way without dividing the gain. For examples of how to divide the gain, see **Home owned separately by one spouse** under **Certain Sales by Married Persons** in Pub. 523.

Sales After May 6, 1997

If you sold your main home after May 6, 1997, you may be able to:

- Exclude all or part of the gain from the sale (see **Exclusion for Sales After May 6, 1997** next), or
- Elect to take the one-time exclusion for people age 55 or older or to postpone paying tax on all or part of the gain (see **Election To Use Rules That Apply To Sales Before May 7, 1997** on this page), or
- Elect to pay tax on all the gain. To do so, complete all the lines in Part I that apply to you other than line 2. Enter the gain from line 8 on Schedule D (Form 1040).

Exclusion for Sales After May 6, 1997

You can exclude up to $250,000 ($500,000 for certain married persons filing a joint return) of gain from the sale of your main home if **both 1** and **2** below apply.

1. Neither you nor your spouse if filing a joint return are excluding gain from the sale of another home after May 6, 1997.

2. You or your spouse if filing a joint return owned and lived in the home for periods adding up to at least 2 years within the 5-year period ending on the date of sale. But see **Exceptions To the Use Test** and **Exceptions To the Ownership and Use Tests** on this page.

If both **1** and **2** do not apply, you may still be able to exclude all or part of the gain. See **Reduced exclusion** on page 5 for details.

To take the exclusion, complete Part IV. If the gain is less than the maximum exclusion entered on line 25, the difference cannot be excluded on a future sale of another main home. For more details on this exclusion, see Pub. 523.

Exceptions To the Use Test

The following exceptions apply in determining the time you lived in the home sold.

Temporary absences. You can count short temporary absences such as for vacations or other seasonal absences as time lived in the home even if you rented out the home during the absences.

Individuals with a disability. If you meet this exception, you are treated as having lived in the home sold during any time that you lived in a facility such as a nursing home. The facility must be licensed by a state or political subdivision to care for persons with your condition. You meet this exception if, during the 5-year period ending on the date of sale—

- You became physically or mentally unable to care for yourself, and
- You owned and lived in your home as your main home for a total of at least 1 year.

Divorced or separated taxpayers. You may be able to count time your spouse or former spouse was allowed to live in the home. See Pub. 523 for details.

Exceptions To the Ownership and Use Tests

The following exceptions apply in determining the time you owned and lived in the home sold.

Surviving spouse. If your spouse died before the old home was sold and you have not remarried, you are treated as having owned and lived in the home sold during any time that your deceased spouse owned and lived in the home.

Home transferred from spouse or former spouse. You may be able to count time your spouse or former spouse owned and lived in the home. See Pub. 523 for details.

Home sold before 1997. You may be able to count time you owned and lived in a previous home on which you postponed all or part of the gain, or that was destroyed or condemned. See Pub. 523 for details.

Election To Use Rules That Apply To Sales Before May 7, 1997

If you sold your home after May 6, 1997, you can elect to use the rules, explained on page 2, that apply to sales before May 7, 1997. You can make the election if **any** of the following apply:

- You sold your home **before** August 6, 1997.
- You sold your home **after** August 5, 1997, under a contract that was binding on that date.
- You sold your home **after** August 5, 1997, **and** you bought a new home on or before that date, or under a binding contract that was in effect on that date, and that purchase would qualify you to postpone gain on the sale. See **Postponing Gain** on page 2 for details.

To make the election for this sale, complete Part II and/or Part III.

Which Parts To Complete

Part I. All filers must complete Part I.

Part II. Complete this part only if you qualify for the **One-Time Exclusion for People Age 55 or Older** and you want to make the election for this sale.

Part III. If you are using the rules that apply to sales before May 7, 1997, complete line 15 even if you did not take the exclusion in Part II. Complete lines 16 through 23 only if line 15 is more than zero and you checked the "Yes" box on line 2.

Part IV. Complete this part only if you sold your main home after May 6, 1997, and you do not qualify for and elect to use the rules that apply to sales before May 7, 1997.

Specific Instructions

Address

If you are filing Form 2119 by itself and not with your tax return, enter your address on page 1 of the form and complete the signature area on page 2.

Line 1

Enter the date of sale. If you received a **Form 1099-S,** Proceeds From Real Estate Transactions, the date should be shown in box 1. If you did not receive a Form 1099-S, the date of sale is the earlier of **(a)** the date the title transferred, or **(b)** the date the economic burdens and benefits of ownership shifted to the buyer.

If you sold your home **after** May 6, 1997, new rules apply. See **Sales After May 6, 1997** on this page for details. Complete line 2 only if you qualify for and elect to use the rules that apply to sales before May 7, 1997.

Line 3

Old home. If part of your old main home was rented out or used for business and in the year of sale you **were not** entitled to deduct expenses for the part that was rented or used for business, report the entire sale on Form 2119.

If you **were** entitled to deduct expenses in the year of sale for the part that was rented or used for business, treat the sale as two separate sales. Report on Form 4797 the part of the sale that applies to the rental or business use. Report on Form 2119 only the part of the sale that represents your main home. You must allocate between Forms 2119 and 4797 the sales price, expenses of sale, and the adjusted basis of the property sold. Attach a statement showing the total selling price of the property and the method used to allocate the amounts between the two forms.

You cannot postpone the part of the gain that is reported on Form 4797. But you may be able to take the one-time exclusion for people age 55 or older or the exclusion for sales after May 6, 1997, on that part of the gain. You can take the exclusion if you otherwise qualify and the rental or business use did not exceed 2 years (3 years for the exclusion applicable to sales after May 6, 1997) of the 5-year period ending on the date of sale. To do so, allocate any allowable exclusion between Forms 2119 and 4797. Attach a statement showing the total exclusion and the method used to allocate it between the two forms. Enter on Form 2119, line 14 or line 27, whichever applies, only the part of the total exclusion that applies to your main home. On the dotted line next to line 14 or line 27, write "Allocated." For details on how to report the part of the exclusion that applies to the rental or business use, see **Special Rules** in the Form 4797 instructions.

For more details on a home used partly for business or rental, see Pub. 523.

Note: Only the part of the fixing-up expenses that applies to your main home may be included on line 16. These expenses are not allowed on Form 4797.

New home. If part of your new main home is rented out or used for business and you are completing Part III of Form 2119, enter on line 19b only the part of the total cost of the property that is allocable to your new main home. Attach a statement showing the total cost of the property and the allocation between the part that is your new main home and the part that is rented out or used for business. For an example, see Pub. 523.

Line 4

Enter the selling price of your old home. Generally, this includes the amount of money you received, plus all notes, mortgages, or other debts that are part of the sale. If you received a Form 1099-S, the total of these items should be shown in box 2. The selling price also includes the fair market value of any other property or services you received as part of the sale. If you received any other property or services as part of the sale, the value of these items is not shown on Form 1099-S. However, box 4 of that form should be checked.

Do not include amounts you received for personal property sold with your home. Personal property is property that is not a permanent part of the home. Examples are furniture, draperies, and lawn equipment.

Line 5

Enter the total expenses you paid to sell your old home. These expenses include commissions, advertising, attorney and legal fees, appraisal fees, title insurance, transfer and stamp taxes, and recording fees. Loan charges, such as points charged to the seller, are also selling expenses. **Do not** include fixing-up expenses on this line. Instead, if you are completing Part III, see the instructions for line 16 on this page.

Line 7

Use the worksheet on this page to figure the adjusted basis of the home you sold. But if any of the following situations apply, see **Table 1** in Pub. 523 before using the worksheet.

- You are a surviving spouse and you owned your old home jointly with your deceased spouse.
- You built your old home and did not file a Form 2119 to postpone gain on the sale of a previous home.
- You acquired your old home other than by purchase, such as by gift, inheritance, or trade.
- Your old home was damaged as a result of a casualty.

Seller-paid points. You must subtract any points the seller paid from the purchase price of your old main home if **(1)** you bought the home after April 3, 1994, **or (2)** you bought the home after 1990 but before April 4, 1994, and you deducted the seller-paid points.

You must also subtract any points the seller paid from the purchase price of your new main home if you are completing Part III and either **(1)** or **(2)** above applies.

For details on points, see **Pub. 936,** Home Mortgage Interest Deduction.

Settlement fees or closing costs. Certain expenses you incurred to buy your home increase your basis. These expenses should be shown on your settlement statement. For more details, see Pub. 523.

Adjusted Basis of Home Sold Worksheet—Line 7 (keep for your records)

Caution: *If any of the situations listed in the instructions for line 7 apply to you, see **Table 1** in Pub. 523 before you use this worksheet.*

1.	Enter the purchase price of your old home. But if you filed Form 2119 when you originally acquired your old home to postpone gain on the sale of a previous home, enter the adjusted basis of the new home from that Form 2119		**1.** ______
2.	Seller-paid points, for home bought after 1990 (see this page). **Do not** include any seller-paid points you previously subtracted to arrive at the amount entered on line 1 above		**2.** ______
3.	Subtract line 2 from line 1		**3.** ______
4.	Settlement fees or closing costs (see this page). **Do not** include amounts previously deducted as moving expenses. If line 1 includes the adjusted basis of the new home from Form 2119, skip lines 4a–5 and go to line 6.		
a.	Abstract and recording fees	**4a.** ______	
b.	Legal fees (including title search and preparing documents)	**4b.** ______	
c.	Surveys	**4c.** ______	
d.	Title insurance	**4d.** ______	
e.	Transfer or stamp taxes	**4e.** ______	
f.	Amounts the seller owed that you agreed to pay, such as back taxes or interest, recording or mortgage fees, and sales commissions	**4f.** ______	
g.	Other	**4g.** ______	
5.	Add lines 4a through 4g		**5.** ______
6.	Cost of capital improvements from the worksheet on page 6. **Do not** include any capital improvements included on line 1 above		**6.** ______
7.	Special tax assessments paid on your old home for local improvements such as streets and sidewalks		**7.** ______
8.	Other increases to basis		**8.** ______
9.	Add lines 3, 5, 6, 7, and 8		**9.** ______
10.	Depreciation, related to the business use or rental of your old home, claimed (or allowable) on prior year tax returns	**10.** ______	
11.	Residential energy credit (generally allowed from 1977 through 1987) and adoption credit claimed for any capital improvements included on line 6 and, if applicable, line 1 above	**11.** ______	
12.	Payments received for any easement or right-of-way granted	**12.** ______	
13.	Other decreases to basis	**13.** ______	
14.	Add lines 10 through 13		**14.** ______
15.	**Adjusted basis of home sold.** Subtract line 14 from line 9. Enter the result here and on Form 2119, line 7		**15.** ______

Line 15

If you report the gain from the sale of your home on Form 6252 using the installment method, first complete the lines on Form 2119 that apply to you. If you completed line 14 or line 22 of Form 2119, enter the total of those lines on line 15 of Form 6252. If you completed line 27 of Form 2119, enter that amount on line 15 of Form 6252. Otherwise, enter zero on line 15 of Form 6252. Do not enter the gain from Form 2119 on Schedule D (Form 1040).

Line 16

Enter the fixing-up expenses you paid to help sell your old home. Fixing-up expenses are decorating and repair costs. For example, the cost of painting the home, planting flowers, and replacing broken windows are fixing-up expenses. However, to qualify, the expenses must be:

• For work done during the 90-day period ending on the day you signed the contract to sell your home (not the day you signed the listing contract with the real estate company), and

• Paid no later than 30 days after the date of sale.

Fixing-up expenses do not include amounts paid for capital improvements. Instead, add these amounts to the basis of the property sold. They also do not include selling expenses included on line 5 or amounts that are otherwise deductible.

Line 19b

The cost of your new home includes one or more of the following if paid or incurred within the replacement period (defined on page 1):

• Cash payments,

• The amount of any mortgage or other debt on the new home,

• The cost of capital improvements, or

• Any other expenses that must be added to the basis of the new home.

If you bought your new home, you may have to reduce the cost of your home by any points the seller paid. See **Seller-paid points** on page 4.

If you built your new home, include the cost of the land and all construction costs incurred within the replacement period. Do not include the cost of land purchased before or after the replacement period or land acquired other than by purchase. Also, do not include the value of your own labor.

Note: *If line 21 of Form 2119 shows a taxable gain and you incur costs for capital improvements made after you file it but within the replacement period, you should refigure your taxable gain. If the refigured taxable gain is less than the gain you originally reported, file Form 1040X to correct your 1997 tax return.*

Line 23

Subtract line 22 from 19b. This is your adjusted basis in your new home. But if you built your new home and the land is not included in the amount entered on line 19b, your adjusted basis in your new home is the amount on line 23 plus the adjusted basis of the land.

Line 25

If you checked the "No" box on line 24, see **Reduced exclusion** on this page for the amount to enter.

If you checked the "Yes" box on line 24, enter $250,000 ($500,000 if married filing a joint return **and** both you and your spouse lived in the home for a total of at least 2 years within the 5-year period ending on the date of sale). But see **Reduced exclusion** on this page for the amount to enter if:

• You (or your spouse if filing a joint return) are excluding gain on the sale of another home after May 6, 1997, **or**

• You are married filing a joint return but you are not eligible to enter $500,000 on line 25 because both you and your spouse did not live in the home for the required period.

Reduced exclusion. Use the worksheet on this page to figure the amount to enter on line 25 if **either 1** or **2** below applies.

1. You (or your spouse if filing a joint return) owned the home on August 5, 1997, and sold it after that date.

2. Because of a change in health or place of employment, you (or your spouse if filing a joint return):

a. Did not own or live in the home for a total of at least 2 years within the 5-year period ending on the date of sale, or

b. Are excluding gain on the sale of another home after May 6, 1997.

If neither **1** nor **2** applies, **do not** use the **Reduced Exclusion Worksheet** on this page. Instead, if you checked the "No" box on line 24, enter zero on line 25. If you checked the "Yes" box on line 24, enter $250,000 on line 25.

Reduced Exclusion Worksheet—Line 25 (keep for your records)

Caution: *Complete column (b) only if you are married filing a joint return.*		**(a) You**	**(b) Your spouse**
1. Maximum amount	1.	$250,000	$250,000
2. During the 5-year period ending on the date of sale, enter the **smaller** of: • The number of days each person used the property as a main home, or • The number of days each person owned the property. If married filing jointly and one spouse owned the property longer than the other spouse, both spouses are treated as owning the property for the longer period.	2.		
3. Are you (or your spouse if filing jointly) excluding gain from the sale of another home after May 6, 1997? **No.** Skip line 3 and enter the number of days from line 2 on line 4. **Yes.** If the other home was sold before this home, enter the number of days between the date of sale of the other home and the date of sale of this home. Otherwise, skip line 3 and enter the number of days from line 2 on line 4	3.		
4. Enter the **smaller** of line 2 or line 3	4.		
5. Divide line 4 by 730 days and enter the result as a decimal.	5.		
6. Multiply line 1 by the decimal amount on line 5.	6.		
7. Add the amounts in columns (a) and (b) of line 6. Enter the result here and on Form 2119, line 25.			7.

Capital Improvements Worksheet (keep for your records)

These are improvements made to your home that add to its value, prolong its useful life, or adapt it to new uses. Examples are listed below.

Caution: *Do not include improvements that are no longer part of your main home. For example, if you put wall-to-wall carpeting in your home and later replaced it with new wall-to-wall carpeting, do not include the cost of the first carpeting as a capital improvement.*

(a) Type of Improvement	(b) Year	(c) Amount
Additions		
Bedroom		
Bathroom		
Deck		
Garage		
Porch		
Patio		
Storage shed		
Fireplace		
Other		
Lawn & Grounds		
Landscaping		
Driveway		
Walkway		
Fence		
Retaining wall		
Sprinkler system		
Swimming pool		
Exterior lighting		
Other		
Communications		
Satellite dish		
Intercom		
Security system		
Other		
Miscellaneous		
Storm windows and doors		
Roof		
Central vacuum		
Other		

(a) Type of Improvement	(b) Year	(c) Amount
Heating & Air Conditioning		
Heating system		
Central air conditioning		
Furnace		
Duct work		
Central humidifier		
Filtration system		
Other		
Electrical		
Light fixtures		
Wiring upgrades		
Other		
Plumbing		
Water heater		
Soft water system		
Filtration system		
Other		
Insulation		
Attic		
Walls		
Floors		
Pipes and duct work		
Other		
Interior Improvements		
Built-in appliances		
Kitchen modernization		
Bathroom modernization		
Flooring		
Wall-to-wall carpeting		
Other		

Total capital improvements. Add the amounts in column **(c).** Enter the total here and on line 6 of the **Adjusted Basis of Home Sold Worksheet** on page 4. . . . . $ ________

Paperwork Reduction Act Notice. We ask for the information on this form to carry out the Internal Revenue laws of the United States. You are required to give us the information. We need it to ensure that you are complying with these laws and to allow us to figure and collect the right amount of tax.

You are not required to provide the information requested on a form that is subject to the Paperwork Reduction Act unless the form displays a valid OMB control number. Books or records relating to a form or its instructions must be retained as long as their contents may become material in the administration of any Internal Revenue law. Generally, tax returns and return information are confidential, as required by Internal Revenue Code section 6103.

The time needed to complete and file this form will vary depending on individual circumstances. The estimated average time is: **Recordkeeping,** 46 min.; **Learning about the law or the form,** 20 min.; **Preparing the form,** 1 hr., 54 min.; and **Copying, assembling, and sending the form to the IRS,** 25 min.

If you have comments concerning the accuracy of these time estimates or suggestions for making this form simpler, we would be happy to hear from you. See the Instructions for Form 1040.

1997

Department of the Treasury
Internal Revenue Service

Instructions for Form 4562

Depreciation and Amortization (Including Information on Listed Property)

Section references are to the Internal Revenue Code unless otherwise noted.

Changes To Note

• For tax years beginning in 1997, the maximum section 179 expense deduction has been increased to $18,000 ($38,000 for enterprise zone businesses).

• Any qualified rent-to-own property placed in service after August 5, 1997, is classified as 3-year property under the General Depreciation System and has a 4-year class life under the Alternative Depreciation System. Generally, qualified rent-to-own property is tangible personal property of a type used within the home for personal use and held by a dealer for lease to customers under a rent-to-own agreement. See section 168(i)(14) for more details.

• For property placed in service after August 5, 1997, the use of the income forecast method is limited to motion picture films, videotapes, sound recordings, copyrights, books, and patents. You cannot use this method to depreciate any amortizable section 197 intangible.

• For property placed in service after August 5, 1997, the limits on depreciation and the section 179 expense deduction that apply solely to passenger automobiles have been **(a)** eliminated for the cost of installed qualified clean-fuel vehicle property and **(b)** tripled for certain electric vehicles. See page 8 for more details.

General Instructions

Purpose of Form

Use Form 4562 to claim your deduction for depreciation and amortization; to make the election to expense certain tangible property (section 179); and to provide information on the business/investment use of automobiles and other listed property.

Who Must File

Except as otherwise noted, complete and file Form 4562 if you are claiming any of the following.

• Depreciation for property placed in service during the 1997 tax year.

• A section 179 expense deduction (which may include a carryover from a previous year).

• Depreciation on any vehicle or other listed property (regardless of when it was placed in service).

• A deduction for any vehicle reported on a form other than **Schedule C (Form 1040),** Profit or Loss From Business, or **Schedule C-EZ (Form 1040),** Net Profit From Business.

• Any depreciation on a corporate income tax return (other than Form 1120S).

• Amortization of costs that begins during the 1997 tax year.

However, **do not** file Form 4562 to report depreciation and information on the use of vehicles if you are an employee deducting job-related vehicle expenses using either the standard mileage rate or actual expenses. Instead, use **Form 2106,** Employee Business Expenses, or **Form 2106-EZ,** Unreimbursed Employee Business Expenses, for this purpose.

Submit a separate Form 4562 for each business or activity on your return. If you need more space, attach additional sheets. However, complete only one Part I in its entirety when computing your allowable section 179 expense deduction.

Definitions

Depreciation

Depreciation is the annual deduction allowed to recover the cost or other basis of business or income-producing property with a determinable useful life of more than 1 year. However, land is not depreciable.

Depreciation starts when you first use the property in your business or for the production of income. It ends when you take the property out of service, deduct all your depreciable cost or other basis, or no longer use the property in your business or for the production of income.

Amortization

Amortization is similar to the straight line method of depreciation in that an annual deduction is allowed to recover certain costs over a fixed time period. You can amortize such items as the costs of starting a business, goodwill and certain other intangibles, reforestation, and pollution control facilities. For additional information, get **Pub. 535,** Business Expenses.

Listed Property

Listed property generally includes:

• Passenger automobiles weighing 6,000 pounds or less.

• Any other property used for transportation if the nature of the property lends itself to personal use, such as motorcycles, pick-up trucks, etc.

• Any property used for entertainment or recreational purposes (such as photographic, phonographic, communication, and video recording equipment).

• Cellular telephones (or other similar telecommunications equipment).

• Computers or peripheral equipment.

Exception. Listed property does not include **(a)** photographic, phonographic, communication, or video equipment used exclusively in a taxpayer's trade or business or at the taxpayer's regular business establishment; **(b)** any computer or peripheral equipment used exclusively at a regular business establishment and owned or leased by the person operating the establishment; or **(c)** an ambulance, hearse, or vehicle used for transporting persons or property for hire. For purposes of the preceding sentence, a portion of the taxpayer's home is treated as a regular business establishment only if that portion meets the requirements under section 280A(c)(1) for deducting expenses attributable to the business use of a home. However, for any property listed under **(a)** above, the regular business establishment of an employee is his or her employer's regular business establishment.

Recordkeeping

Except for Part V (relating to listed property), the IRS does not require you to submit detailed information with your return on the depreciation of assets placed in service in previous tax years. However, the information needed to compute your depreciation deduction (basis, method, etc.) must be part of your permanent records.

Because Form 4562 does not provide for permanent recordkeeping, you may use the depreciation worksheet on page 12 to assist you in maintaining depreciation records. However, the worksheet is designed only for Federal income tax purposes. You may need to keep additional records for accounting and state income tax purposes.

Specific Instructions

Part I

Caution: *An estate or trust cannot make this election.*

You may elect to expense part of the cost of certain tangible personal property used in your trade or business and certain other property described in section 1245(a)(3). To do so, you must have:

- Purchased the property (as defined in section 179(d)(2)) and
- Placed it in service during the 1997 tax year.

You must make the election with:

1. The original return you file for the tax year the property was placed in service (whether or not you file your return on time), or

2. An amended return filed no later than the due date (including extensions) for your return for the tax year the property was placed in service.

Once made, the election (and the selection of the property you elect to expense) may not be revoked without IRS consent.

If you elect this deduction, reduce the amount on which you figure your depreciation or amortization deduction by the section 179 expense deduction.

Section 179 property does **not** include:

1. Property used 50% or less in your trade or business.

2. Property held for investment (section 212 property).

3. Property you lease to others as a noncorporate lessor **unless (a)** you manufactured or produced the property or **(b)** the term of the lease is less than 50% of the property's class life, and for the first 12 months after the property is transferred to the lessee, the sum of the deductions related to the property that are allowed to you **solely** under section 162 (except rents and reimbursed amounts) is more than 15% of the rental income from the property.

4. Property used mainly outside the United States (except for property described in section 168(g)(4)).

5. Property used for lodging or for furnishing the lodging (except as provided in section 50(b)(2)).

6. Property used by a tax-exempt organization (other than a section 521 farmers' cooperative) unless the property is used mainly in a taxable unrelated trade or business.

7. Property used by a governmental unit or foreign person or entity (except for property used under a lease with a term of less than 6 months).

8. Air conditioning or heating units.

The section 179 expense deduction is subject to two separate limitations: a dollar limitation and a taxable income limitation. Both limitations are figured in Part I.

For a partnership, these limitations apply to the partnership and each partner. For an S corporation, these limitations apply to the S corporation and each shareholder. For a controlled group, all component members are treated as one taxpayer.

For more details on the section 179 expense deduction, see **Pub. 946,** How To Depreciate Property.

Line 1

For an enterprise zone business, the maximum section 179 expense deduction of $18,000 is increased by the **smaller** of:

- $20,000 or
- The cost of section 179 property that is also qualified zone property (including such property placed in service by your spouse, even if you are filing a separate return).

Cross out the preprinted entry on line 1 and enter in the margin the larger amount if your business is an enterprise zone business. For the definitions of enterprise zone business and qualified zone property, see sections 1397B and 1397C.

Recapture Rule: *If any qualified zone property placed in service during the current year ceases to be used in an empowerment zone by an enterprise zone business in a later year, the benefit of the increased section 179 expense deduction must be reported as "other income" on your return.*

Line 2

Enter the cost of all section 179 property placed in service during the tax year. Include amounts from any listed property from Part V. Also include any section 179 property placed in service by your spouse, even if you are filing a separate return.

For an enterprise zone business, include on this line only 50% of the cost of section 179 property that is also qualified zone property.

Line 5

If line 5 is zero, you cannot elect to expense any property. Skip lines 6 through 11, enter zero on line 12, and enter the carryover of any disallowed deduction from 1996 on line 13.

If you are married filing separately, you and your spouse must allocate the dollar limitation for the tax year. To do so, multiply the total limitation that you would otherwise enter on line 5 by 50%, unless you both elect a different allocation. If you both elect a different allocation, multiply the total limitation by the percentage elected. The sum of the percentages you and your spouse elect must equal 100%. **Do not** enter on line 5 more than your share of the total dollar limitation.

Line 6

Caution: ***Do not*** *include any listed property on line 6.*

Column (a). Enter a brief description of the property for which you are making the election (e.g., truck, office furniture, etc.).

Column (b). Enter the cost of the property. If you acquired the property through a trade-in, **do not** include any undepreciated basis of the assets you traded in. See **Pub. 551,** Basis of Assets, for more details.

Column (c). Enter the amount you elect to expense. You do not have to expense the entire cost of the property. You can depreciate the amount you do not expense. See the line 15 and line 16 instructions.

To report your share of a section 179 expense deduction from a partnership or an S corporation, write "from Schedule K-1 (Form 1065)" or "from Schedule K-1 (Form 1120S)" across columns (a) and (b).

Line 10

The carryover of disallowed deduction from 1996 is the amount of section 179 property, if any, you elected to expense in previous years, but not allowed as a deduction due to the business income limitation. If you filed Form 4562 for 1996, enter the amount from line 13 of your 1996 Form 4562. For additional details, see Pub. 946.

Line 11

The section 179 expense deduction is further limited to the "business income" limitation under section 179(b)(3).

For purposes of the rules that follow:

- If you have to apply another Code section that has a limitation based on taxable income, see Regulations section 1.179-2(c)(5) for rules on how to apply the business income limitation under section 179 in such a case.
- You are considered to **actively conduct** a trade or business if you meaningfully participate in its management or operations. A mere passive investor is not considered to actively conduct a trade or business.

Individuals. Enter the smaller of line 5 or the aggregate taxable income from any trade or business you actively conducted, computed without regard to any section 179 expense deduction, the deduction for one-half of self-employment taxes under section 164(f), or any net operating loss deduction. Include in aggregate taxable income the wages, salaries, tips, and other compensation you earned as an employee (not reduced by unreimbursed employee business expenses). If you are married filing a joint return, combine the aggregate taxable incomes for you and your spouse.

Partnerships. Enter the smaller of line 5 or the aggregate of the partnership's items of income and expense described in section 702(a) from any trade or business the partnership actively conducted (other than credits, tax-exempt income, the section 179 expense deduction, and guaranteed payments under section 707(c)).

S corporations. Enter the smaller of line 5 or the aggregate of the corporation's items of income and expense described in section 1366(a) from any trade or business the corporation actively conducted (other than credits, tax-exempt income, the section 179 expense deduction, and the deduction for compensation paid to the corporation's shareholder-employees).

Corporations other than S corporations. Enter the smaller of line 5 or the corporation's taxable income before the section 179 expense deduction, net operating loss deduction, and special deductions (excluding items not derived from a trade or business actively conducted by the corporation).

Line 12

The limitations on lines 5 and 11 apply to the taxpayer, and not to each separate business or activity. Therefore, if you have more than one business or activity, you may allocate your allowable section 179 expense deduction among them.

To do so, write "Summary" at the top of Part I of the separate Form 4562 you are completing for the aggregate amounts from all businesses or activities. **Do not** complete the rest of that form. On line 12 of the Form 4562 you prepare for each separate business or activity, enter the amount allocated to the business or activity from the "Summary." No other entry is required in Part I of the separate Form 4562 prepared for each business or activity.

Part II

The term "Modified Accelerated Cost Recovery System" (MACRS) includes the General Depreciation System and the Alternative Depreciation System. Generally, MACRS is used to depreciate any tangible property placed in service after 1986. However, MACRS does not apply to films, videotapes, and sound recordings. See section 168(f) for other exceptions. For more details on MACRS, see Pub. 946. For information on other methods of depreciation, see **Pub. 534,** Depreciating Property Placed In Service Before 1987.

Depreciation may be an adjustment for alternative minimum tax purposes. For details, see **Form 4626,** Alternative Minimum Tax—Corporations; **Form 6251,** Alternative Minimum Tax—Individuals; or Schedule I of **Form 1041,** U.S. Income Tax Return for Estates and Trusts.

Section A

Line 14

To simplify the computation of MACRS depreciation, you may elect to group assets into one or more general asset accounts under section 168(i)(4). The assets in each general asset account are depreciated as a single asset.

Each account must include only assets that were placed in service during the same tax year with the same asset class (if any), depreciation method, recovery period, and convention. However, an asset cannot be included in a general asset account if the asset is used both for personal purposes and business/investment purposes.

When an asset in an account is disposed of, the amount realized generally must be recognized as ordinary income. The unadjusted depreciable basis and depreciation reserve of the general asset account are not affected as a result of a disposition.

Special rules apply to passenger automobiles, assets generating foreign source income, assets converted to personal use, and certain asset dispositions. For more details, see Regulations section 1.168(i)-1.

To make the election, check the box on line 14. You must make the election on your return filed no later than the due date (including extensions) for the tax year in which the assets included in the general asset account were placed in service. Once made, the election is irrevocable and applies to the tax year for which the election is made and all later tax years.

Section B

Lines 15a Through 15i

Use lines 15a through 15i only for assets placed in service during the tax year beginning in 1997 and depreciated under the General Depreciation System, except for automobiles and other listed property (which are reported in Part V).

Column (a). Determine which property you acquired and placed in service during the tax year beginning in 1997. Then, sort that property according to its classification (3-year property, 5-year property, etc.) as shown in column (a) of lines 15a through 15i. The classifications for some property are shown below. For property not shown, see **Determining the classification** on this page.

3-year property includes:

- A racehorse that is more than 2 years old at the time it is placed in service.
- Any horse (other than a racehorse) that is more than 12 years old at the time it is placed in service.
- Any qualified rent-to-own property (as defined in section 168(i)(14)) placed in service after August 5, 1997.

5-year property includes:

- Automobiles.
- Light general purpose trucks.
- Typewriters, calculators, copiers, and duplicating equipment.
- Any semi-conductor manufacturing equipment.
- Any computer or peripheral equipment.
- Any section 1245 property used in connection with research and experimentation.
- Certain energy property specified in section 168(e)(3)(B)(vi).

7-year property includes:

- Office furniture and equipment.
- Appliances, carpets, furniture, etc., used in residential rental property.
- Railroad track.
- Any property that does not have a class life and is not otherwise classified.

10-year property includes:

- Vessels, barges, tugs, and similar water transportation equipment.
- Any single purpose agricultural or horticultural structure (see section 168(i)(13)).
- Any tree or vine bearing fruit or nuts.

15-year property includes:

- Any municipal wastewater treatment plant.
- Any telephone distribution plant and comparable equipment used for 2-way exchange of voice and data communications.
- Any section 1250 property that is a retail motor fuels outlet (whether or not food or other convenience items are sold there).

20-year property includes:

- Farm buildings (other than single purpose agricultural or horticultural structures).
- Municipal sewers not classified as 25-year property.

25-year property is water utility property, which is:

- Property that is an integral part of the gathering, treatment, or commercial distribution of water, that, without regard to this classification, would be 20-year property.
- Municipal sewers. This classification applies to property placed in service after June 12, 1996, except for property placed in service under a binding contract in effect at all times since June 9, 1996.

Residential rental property is a building in which 80% or more of the total rent is from dwelling units.

Nonresidential real property is any real property that is neither residential rental property nor property with a class life of less than 27.5 years.

50-year property includes any improvements necessary to construct or improve a roadbed or right-of-way for railroad track that qualifies as a railroad grading or tunnel bore under section 168(e)(4).

There is no separate line to report 50-year property. Therefore, attach a statement showing the same information as required in columns (a) through (g). Include the deduction in the line 21 "Total" and write "See attachment" in the bottom margin of the form.

Determining the classification. If your depreciable property is **not** listed above, determine the classification as follows.

1. Find the property's class life. See the Table of Class Lives and Recovery Periods in Pub. 946.

2. Use the following table to find the classification in column (b) that corresponds to the class life of the property in column (a).

(a) Class life (in years) (See Pub. 946)	(b) Classification
4 or less	3-year property
More than 4 but less than 10	5-year property
10 or more but less than 16	7-year property
16 or more but less than 20	10-year property
20 or more but less than 25	15-year property
25 or more	20-year property

Column (b). For lines 15h and 15i, enter the month and year you placed the property in service. If you converted property held for personal use to use in a trade or business or for the production of income, treat the property as being placed in service on the conversion date.

Column (c). To find the basis for depreciation, multiply the cost or other basis of the property by the percentage of business/investment use. From that result, subtract any section 179 expense deduction, deduction for removal of barriers to the disabled and the elderly, disabled access credit, and enhanced oil recovery credit. See section 50(c) to determine the basis adjustment for investment credit property.

Column (d). Determine the recovery period from the table on page 5, unless either **1** or **2** below applies.

1. You make an irrevocable election to use the 150% declining balance method of depreciation for 3-, 5-, 7-, or 10-year property (excluding any tree or vine bearing fruit or nuts). The election applies to all property within the classification for which it is made that was placed in service during the tax year. If you elect this method, you must use the recovery period under the Alternative Depreciation System (ADS) discussed in the line 16 instructions. You will not have an adjustment for alternative minimum tax purposes on the property for which you make this election.

2. You acquired qualified Indian reservation property (as defined in section 168(j)(4)). Qualified Indian reservation property does not include property placed in service to conduct class I, II, or III gaming activities. The table for qualified Indian reservation property can be found in Pub. 946.

Recovery Period for Most Property

In the case of:	The recovery period is:
3-year property	3 yrs.
5-year property	5 yrs.
7-year property	7 yrs.
10-year property	10 yrs.
15-year property	15 yrs.
20-year property	20 yrs.
25-year property	25 yrs.
Residential rental property	27.5 yrs.
Nonresidential real property placed in service before May 13, 1993	31.5 yrs.
Nonresidential real property placed in service after May 12, 1993	*39 yrs.
Railroad gradings and tunnel bores	50 yrs.

*The recovery period is 31.5 years for property you placed in service before 1994, if you started construction on the property before May 13, 1993, or you had a binding written contract to buy or build it before that date.

Column (e). The applicable convention determines the portion of the tax year for which depreciation is allowable during a year property is either placed in service or disposed of. There are three types of conventions. To select the correct convention, you must know when you placed the property in service and the type of property.

Half-year convention (HY). This convention applies to all property reported on lines 15a through 15g, unless the mid-quarter convention applies. It does not apply to residential rental property, nonresidential real property, and railroad gradings and tunnel bores. It treats all property placed in service (or disposed of) during any tax year as placed in service (or disposed of) on the midpoint of that tax year.

Mid-quarter convention (MQ). If the aggregate bases of property subject to depreciation under section 168 and placed in service during the last 3 months of your tax year exceed 40% of the aggregate bases of property subject to depreciation under section 168 and placed in service during the entire tax year, the mid-quarter, instead of the half-year, convention applies.

In determining whether the mid-quarter convention applies, **do not** take into account the following:

- Property that is being depreciated under the pre-1987 rules.
- Any residential rental property, nonresidential real property, or railroad gradings and tunnel bores.
- Property that is placed in service and disposed of within the same tax year.

The mid-quarter convention treats all property placed in service (or disposed of) during any quarter as placed in service (or disposed of) on the midpoint of that quarter. However, no depreciation is allowed under this convention for property that is placed in service and disposed of within the same tax year.

Mid-month convention (MM). This convention applies ONLY to residential rental property, nonresidential real property (lines 15h or 15i), and railroad gradings and tunnel bores. It treats all property placed in service (or disposed of) during any month as placed in service (or disposed of) on the midpoint of that month.

Enter "HY" for half-year, "MQ" for mid-quarter, or "MM" for mid-month convention.

Column (f). Applicable depreciation methods are prescribed for each classification of property. Except as otherwise stated below, the applicable method for 3-, 5-, 7-, and 10-year property is the 200% declining balance method, switching to the straight line method in the first tax year that maximizes the depreciation allowance.

For 15- and 20-year property, property used in a farming business, and property for which you elected to use the 150% declining balance method, the applicable method is the 150% declining balance method, switching to the straight line method in the first tax year that maximizes the depreciation allowance.

For water utility property, residential rental property, nonresidential real property, any railroad grading or tunnel bore, or any tree or vine bearing fruit or nuts, the only applicable method is the straight line method.

You may also make an irrevocable election to use the straight line method for all property within a classification that is placed in service during the tax year.

Enter "200DB" for 200% declining balance, "150DB" for 150% declining balance, or "S/L" for straight line.

Column (g). To compute the depreciation deduction you may use optional Tables A through E, starting on page 10. To do this, multiply the applicable rate from the appropriate table by the property's **unadjusted** basis (column (c)). See Pub. 946 for complete tables. If you disposed of the property during the current tax year, multiply the result by the applicable decimal amount from the tables in step 3 below. Or you may compute the deduction yourself by completing the following steps:

Step 1. Determine the depreciation rate as follows.

- If you are using the 200% or 150% declining balance method in column (f), divide the declining balance rate (use 2.00 for 200 DB or 1.50 for 150 DB) by the number of years in the recovery period in column (d). For example, for property depreciated using the 200 DB method over a recovery period of 5 years, divide 2.00 by 5 for a rate of 40%.

You must switch to the straight line rate in the first year that the straight line rate exceeds the declining balance rate.

- If you are using the straight line method, divide 1.00 by the remaining number of years in the recovery period as of the beginning of the tax year (but not less than one). For example, if there are 6½ years remaining in the recovery period as of the beginning of the year, divide 1.00 by 6.5 for a rate of 15.38%.

Step 2. Multiply the percentage rate determined in Step 1 by the property's unrecovered basis (basis for depreciation (as defined in column (c)) reduced by all prior year's depreciation).

Step 3. For property placed in service or disposed of during the current tax year, multiply the result from Step 2 by the applicable decimal amount from the tables below (based on the convention shown in column (e)).

Half-year (HY) convention	0.5

Mid-quarter (MQ) convention

Placed in service (or disposed of) during the:	Placed in service	Disposed of
1st quarter	0.875	0.125
2nd quarter	0.625	0.375
3rd quarter	0.375	0.625
4th quarter	0.125	0.875

Mid-month (MM) convention

Placed in service (or disposed of) during the:	Placed in service	Disposed of
1st month	0.9583	0.0417
2nd month	0.8750	0.1250
3rd month	0.7917	0.2083
4th month	0.7083	0.2917
5th month	0.6250	0.3750
6th month	0.5417	0.4583
7th month	0.4583	0.5417
8th month	0.3750	0.6250
9th month	0.2917	0.7083
10th month	0.2083	0.7917
11th month	0.1250	0.8750
12th month	0.0417	0.9583

Short tax years. See Pub. 946 for rules on how to compute the depreciation deduction for property placed in service in a short tax year.

Section C

Lines 16a Through 16c

Complete lines 16a through 16c for assets, other than automobiles and other listed property, placed in service ONLY during the tax year beginning in 1997 and depreciated under the Alternative Depreciation System. Report on line 17 depreciation on assets placed in service in prior years.

Under ADS, use the applicable depreciation method, the applicable recovery period, and the applicable convention to compute depreciation.

The following types of property **must** be depreciated under ADS:

- Tangible property used predominantly outside the United States.
- Tax-exempt use property.
- Tax-exempt bond financed property.
- Imported property covered by an executive order of the President of the United States.
- Property used predominantly in a farming business and placed in service during any tax year in which you made an election under section 263A(d)(3).

Instead of depreciating property under GDS (line 15), you may make an irrevocable election with respect to any classification of property for any tax year to use ADS. For residential rental and nonresidential real property, you may make this election separately for each property.

Column (a). Use the following rules to determine the classification of the property under ADS.

Class life. Under ADS, the depreciation deduction for most property is based on the property's class life. See the Table of Class Lives and Recovery Periods in Pub. 946. Use line 16a for all property depreciated under ADS, except property that does not have a class life, residential rental and nonresidential real property, water utility property, and railroad gradings and tunnel bores.

See section 168(g)(3) for special rules for determining the class life for certain property.

12-year property. Use line 16b for property that does not have a class life.

40-year property. Use line 16c for residential rental and nonresidential real property.

Water utility property and railroad gradings and tunnel bores. These assets are 50-year property under ADS. There is no separate line to report 50-year property. Therefore, attach a statement showing the same information required in columns (a) through (g). Include the deduction in the line 21 "Total" and write "See attachment" in the bottom margin of the form.

Column (b). For 40-year property, enter the month and year placed in service or converted to use in a trade or business or for the production of income.

Column (c). See the instructions for line 15, column (c).

Column (d). On line 16a, enter the property's class life.

Column (e). Under ADS, the applicable conventions are the same as those used under GDS. See the instructions for line 15, column (e).

Column (g). Compute the depreciation deduction in the same manner as under GDS, except use the straight line method over the ADS recovery period and use the applicable convention.

Part III

Do not use Part III for automobiles and other listed property. Instead, report this property in Part V on page 2 of Form 4562.

Line 17

For tangible property depreciated under MACRS, enter the GDS and ADS deductions for the current year. To compute the deductions, see the instructions for column (g), line 15.

Line 18

Report property that you elect, under section 168(f)(1), to depreciate under the unit-of-production method or any other method not based on a term of years (other than the retirement-replacement-betterment method).

Attach a separate sheet showing:

- A description of the property and the depreciation method you elect that excludes the property from ACRS or MACRS.
- The depreciable basis (cost or other basis reduced, if applicable, by salvage value, any section 179 expense deduction, deduction for removal of barriers to the disabled and the elderly, disabled access credit, and enhanced oil recovery credit).

See section 50(c) to determine the basis adjustment for investment credit property.

Line 19

Enter the total depreciation you are claiming for the following types of property (except listed property and property subject to a section 168(f)(1) election):

- Accelerated cost recovery system (ACRS) property (pre-1987 rules). See Pub. 534.
- Property placed in service before 1981.
- Certain public utility property, which does not meet certain normalization requirements.
- Certain property acquired from related persons.
- Property acquired in certain nonrecognition transactions.
- Certain sound recordings, movies, and videotapes.
- Property depreciated under the income forecast method. For property placed in service after August 5, 1997, the use of the income forecast method is limited to motion picture films, videotapes, sound recordings, copyrights, books, and patents. You cannot use this method to depreciate any amortizable section 197 intangible. See page 9 for more details on section 197 intangibles.
- Intangible property, other than section 197 intangibles, including:

1. Computer software. Use the straight line method over 36 months.

2. Any right to receive tangible property or services under a contract or granted by a governmental unit (not acquired as part of a business).

3. Any interest in a patent or copyright not acquired as part of a business.

4. Residential mortgage servicing rights. Use the straight line method over 108 months.

See section 167(f) for more details.

Prior years' depreciation, plus current year's depreciation, can never exceed the depreciable basis of the property.

The basis and amounts claimed for depreciation should be part of your permanent books and records. **No attachment is necessary.**

Part IV

Line 21

A partnership or S corporation does not include any section 179 expense deduction (line 12) on this line. Any section 179 expense deduction is passed through separately to the partners and shareholders on the appropriate line of their Schedules K-1.

Line 22

If you are subject to the uniform capitalization rules of section 263A, enter the increase in basis from costs you must capitalize. For a detailed discussion of who is subject to these rules, which costs must be capitalized, and allocation of costs among activities, see Regulations section 1.263A-1.

Part V

If you claim the standard mileage rate, actual vehicle expenses (including depreciation), or depreciation on other listed property, you must provide the information requested in Part V, regardless of the tax year the property was placed in service. However, if you file Form 2106, 2106-EZ, or Schedule C-EZ (Form 1040), report this information on that form and not in Part V. Also, if you file Schedule C (Form 1040) and are claiming the standard mileage rate or actual vehicle expenses (except depreciation), and you are not required to file Form 4562 for any other reason, report vehicle information in Part IV of Schedule C and not on Form 4562.

Section A

Lines 24 and 25

Qualified business use. To determine whether to use line 24 or line 25 to report your listed property, you must first determine the percentage of qualified business use for each property. Generally, a qualified business use is any use in your trade or business. However, it does not include any of the following:

- Investment use.
- Leasing the property to a 5% owner or related person.
- The use of the property as compensation for services performed by a 5% owner or related person.
- The use of the property as compensation for services performed by any person (who is not a 5% owner or related person), unless an amount is included in that person's income for the use of the property and, if required, income tax was withheld on that amount.

Exception. If at least 25% of the total use of any aircraft during the tax year is for a qualified business use, the leasing or compensatory use of the aircraft by a 5% owner or related person is treated as a qualified business use.

Determine your percentage of qualified business use similar to the method used to figure the business/investment use percentage in column (c). Your percentage of qualified business use may be smaller than the business/investment use percentage.

For more information, see Pub. 946.

Column (a). List on a property-by-property basis all your listed property in the following order:

1. Automobiles and other vehicles; and

2. Other listed property (computers and peripheral equipment, etc.).

In column (a), list the make and model of automobiles, and give a general description of other listed property.

If you have more than five vehicles used 100% for business/investment purposes, you may group them by tax year. Otherwise, list each vehicle separately.

Column (b). Enter the date the property was placed in service. If property held for personal use is converted to business/investment use, treat the property as placed in service on the date of conversion.

Column (c). Enter the percentage of business/investment use. For automobiles and other vehicles, determine this percentage by dividing the number of miles the vehicle is driven for trade or business purposes or for the production of income during the year (not to include any commuting mileage) by the total number of miles the vehicle is driven for all purposes. Treat vehicles used by employees as being used 100% for business/investment purposes if the value of personal use is included in the employees' gross income, or the employees reimburse the employer for the personal use.

Employers who report the amount of personal use of the vehicle in the employee's gross income, and withhold the appropriate taxes, should enter "100%" for the percentage of business/investment use. For more information, see **Pub. 463,** Travel, Entertainment, Gift, and Car Expenses.

For listed property (such as computers or video equipment), allocate the use based on the most appropriate unit of time the property is actually used. See Temporary Regulations section 1.280F-6T.

If during the tax year you convert property used solely for personal purposes to business/investment use, figure the percentage of business/investment use only for the number of months you use the property in your business or for the production of income. Multiply that percentage by the number of months you use the property in your business or for the production of income, and divide the result by 12.

Column (d). Enter the property's actual cost (including sales tax) or other basis (unadjusted for prior years' depreciation). If you traded in old property, your basis is the adjusted basis of the old property (figured as if 100% of the property's use had been for business/investment purposes) plus any additional amount you paid for the new property.

For a vehicle, reduce your basis by any diesel-powered highway vehicle credit, qualified electric vehicle credit, or deduction for clean-fuel vehicles you claimed.

If you converted the property from personal use to business/investment use, your basis for depreciation is the smaller of the property's adjusted basis or its fair market value on the date of conversion.

Column (e). Multiply column (d) by the percentage in column (c). From that result, subtract any section 179 expense deduction and half of any investment credit taken before 1986 (unless you took the reduced credit).

For automobiles and other listed property placed in service after 1985 (i.e., transition property), reduce the depreciable basis by the entire investment credit.

Column (f). Enter the recovery period. For property placed in service after 1986 and used more than 50% in a qualified business use, use the table in the line 15, column (d) instructions. For property placed in service after 1986 and used 50% or less in a qualified business use, depreciate the property using the straight line method over its ADS recovery period. The ADS recovery period is 5 years for automobiles and computers.

Column (g). Enter the method and convention used to figure your depreciation deduction. See the instructions for line 15, columns (e) and (f). Write "200DB," "150DB," or "S/L," for the depreciation method, and "HY," "MM," or "MQ," for half-year, mid-month, or mid-quarter conventions, respectively. For property placed in service before 1987, write "PRE" if you used the prescribed percentages under ACRS. If you elected an alternate percentage, enter "S/L."

Column (h). See **Limits for passenger automobiles** below before entering an amount in column (h).

For property used more than 50% in a qualified business use (line 24) and placed in service after 1986, figure column (h) by following the instructions for line 15, column (g). If placed in service before 1987, multiply column (e) by the applicable percentage given in Pub. 534 for ACRS property. If the recovery period for an automobile ended before your tax year beginning in 1997, enter your unrecovered basis, if any, in column (h).

For property used 50% or less in a qualified business use (line 25) and placed in service after 1986, figure column (h) by dividing column (e) by column (f) and using the same conventions as discussed in the instructions for line 15, column (e). The amount in column (h) cannot exceed the property's unrecovered basis. If the recovery period for an automobile ended before your tax year beginning in 1997, enter your unrecovered basis, if any, in column (h).

For computers placed in service in a tax year beginning in 1985, multiply column (e) by 4.167%. For computers placed in service in a tax year beginning in 1986, multiply column (e) by 8.333%.

For property placed in service before 1987 that was disposed of during the year, enter zero.

Limits for passenger automobiles. The depreciation deduction plus section 179 expense deduction for passenger automobiles is limited for any tax year.

Definition. "Passenger automobiles" are 4-wheeled vehicles manufactured primarily for use on public roads that are rated at 6,000 pounds unloaded gross vehicle weight or less. For a truck or van, gross vehicle weight is substituted for unloaded gross vehicle weight.

Exception. The following vehicles are not considered passenger automobiles:

- An ambulance, hearse, or combination ambulance-hearse used in your trade or business.
- A vehicle used in your trade or business of transporting persons or property for compensation or hire.

For any passenger automobile you list on line 24 or line 25, the total of columns (h) and (i) for that automobile cannot exceed the limit shown in the tables below. The limit is further reduced when the business/investment use percentage is less than 100%.

Example. If an automobile placed in service in 1997 is used 60% for business/investment purposes, the limit generally is figured as follows: \$3,160 × 60% = \$1,896. However, the \$3,160 limit is increased for certain clean-fuel and electric vehicles. See the footnote below.

For help in figuring the limit, use the **Worksheet for Passenger Automobiles** in Pub. 946.

Limits for Passenger Automobiles Placed in Service Before 1995

IF you placed your automobile in service:	THEN the limit on your depreciation and section 179 expense deduction is:
June 19–Dec. 31, 1984	\$6,000
Jan. 1–Apr. 2, 1985	\$6,200
Apr. 3, 1985–Dec. 31, 1986	\$4,800
Jan. 1. 1987–Dec. 31, 1990	\$1,475
Jan. 1, 1991–Dec. 31, 1992	\$1,575
Jan. 1, 1993–Dec. 31, 1994	\$1,675

Limits for Passenger Automobiles Placed in Service After 1994

IF you placed your automobile in service:	AND the number of tax years in which this automobile has been in service is:	THEN the limit on your depreciation and section 179 expense deduction is:
Jan. 1, 1995–Dec. 31, 1996	1	\$3,060
	2	\$4,900
	3	\$2,950
	4 or more	\$1,775
Jan. 1–Dec. 31, 1997	1	\$3,160 *
	2	\$5,000 *
After Dec. 31, 1997	1	*, **

*For vehicles placed in service after August 5, 1997:

- This limit does not apply to the cost of any qualified clean-fuel vehicle property (such as retrofit parts and components) installed on a vehicle for the purpose of permitting that vehicle to run on a clean-burning fuel. See section 179A for definitions.
- This limit is **tripled** for vehicles produced by an original equipment manufacturer and designed to run primarily on electricity.

**The limit for automobiles placed in service after Dec. 31, 1997, will be published in the Internal Revenue Bulletin. This amount was not available at the time these instructions were printed.

Column (i). Enter the amount you choose to expense for section 179 property used more than 50% in a qualified business use (subject to the limits for passenger automobiles noted above). Refer to the Part I instructions to determine if the property qualifies under section 179. Be sure to include the total cost of such property (50% of the cost if qualified zone property placed in service by an enterprise zone business) on line 2, page 1.

Recapture of depreciation and section 179 expense deduction. For listed property used more than 50% in a qualified business use in the year placed in service and used 50% or less in a later year, you may have to recapture in the later year part of the depreciation and section 179 expense deduction. Use **Form 4797,** Sales of Business Property, to figure the recapture amount.

Section B

Except as noted below, you must complete items 28 through 34 for each vehicle identified in Section A. Employees must provide their employers with the information requested in items 28 through 34 for each automobile or vehicle provided for their use.

Exception. Employers are not required to complete items 28 through 34 for vehicles used by employees who are not more than 5% owners or related persons and for which question 35, 36, 37, 38, or 39 is answered "Yes."

Section C

For employers providing vehicles to their employees, two types of written policy statements will satisfy the employer's substantiation requirements under section 274(d):

- A policy statement that prohibits personal use including commuting, and
- A policy statement that prohibits personal use except for commuting.

An employee does not need to keep a separate set of records for any vehicle that satisfies these written policy statement rules.

Line 35

A policy statement that prohibits personal use (including commuting) must meet **all** of the following conditions:

- The employer owns or leases the vehicle and provides it to one or more employees for use in the employer's trade or business.
- When the vehicle is not used in the employer's trade or business, it is kept on the employer's business premises, unless it is temporarily located elsewhere (e.g., for maintenance or because of a mechanical failure).
- No employee using the vehicle lives at the employer's business premises.
- No employee may use the vehicle for personal purposes, other than de minimis personal use (e.g., a stop for lunch between two business deliveries).
- Except for de minimis use, the employer reasonably believes that no employee uses the vehicle for any personal purpose.

Line 36

A policy statement that prohibits personal use (except for commuting) is **not** available if the commuting employee is an officer, director, or 1% or more owner. This policy must meet **all** of the following conditions:

- The employer owns or leases the vehicle and provides it to one or more employees for use in the employer's trade or business, and it is used in the employer's trade or business.
- For bona fide noncompensatory business reasons, the employer requires the employee to commute to and/or from work in the vehicle.
- The employer establishes a written policy under which the employee may not use the vehicle for personal purposes, other than commuting or de minimis personal use (e.g., a stop for a personal errand between a business delivery and the employee's home).
- Except for de minimis use, the employer reasonably believes that the employee does not use the vehicle for any personal purpose other than commuting.
- The employer accounts for the commuting use by including an appropriate amount in the employee's gross income.

For both written policy statements, there must be evidence that would enable the IRS to determine whether use of the vehicle meets the conditions stated above.

Line 38

An employer that provides more than five vehicles to its employees who are not 5% owners or related persons need not complete Section B for such vehicles. Instead, the employer must obtain the information from its employees and retain the information received.

Line 39

An automobile meets the requirements for qualified demonstration use if the employer maintains a written policy statement that:

- Prohibits its use by individuals other than full-time automobile salesmen.
- Prohibits its use for personal vacation trips.
- Prohibits storage of personal possessions in the automobile.
- Limits the total mileage outside the salesmen's normal working hours.

Part VI

Each year you may elect to deduct part of certain capital costs over a fixed period. If you amortize property, the part you amortize does not qualify for the election to expense certain tangible property or for depreciation.

For individuals reporting amortization of bond premium for bonds acquired before October 23, 1986, **do not** report the deduction here. See the instructions for Schedule A (Form 1040), line 27.

For taxpayers (other than corporations) claiming a deduction for amortization of bond premium for bonds acquired after October 22, 1986, but before January 1, 1988, the deduction is treated as interest expense and is subject to the investment interest limitations. Use **Form 4952,** Investment Interest Expense Deduction, to compute the allowable deduction.

For taxable bonds acquired after 1987, the amortization offsets the interest income. See **Pub. 550,** Investment Income and Expenses.

Line 40

Complete line 40 only for those costs for which the amortization period begins during your tax year beginning in 1997.

Column (a). Describe the costs you are amortizing. You may amortize:

- Pollution control facilities (section 169, limited by section 291 for corporations).
- Certain bond premiums (section 171).
- Research and experimental expenditures (section 174).
- The cost of acquiring a lease (section 178).
- Qualified forestation and reforestation costs (section 194).
- Business start-up expenditures (section 195).
- Organizational expenditures for a corporation (section 248) or partnership (section 709).
- Optional write-off of certain tax preferences over the period specified in section 59(e).
- Certain section 197 intangibles, which generally include the following:

1. Goodwill.

2. Going concern value.

3. Workforce in place.

4. Business books and records, operating systems, or any other information base.

5. Any patent, copyright, formula, process, design, pattern, know how, format, or similar item.

6. Any customer-based intangible (e.g., composition of market or market share).

7. Any supplier-based intangible.

8. Any license, permit, or other right granted by a governmental unit.

9. Any covenant not to compete entered into in connection with the acquisition of a business.

10. Any franchise (other than a sports franchise), trademark, or trade name.

Section 197 intangibles must be amortized over 15 years starting with the month the intangibles were acquired.

Column (b). Enter the date the amortization period begins under the applicable Code section.

Column (c). Enter the total amount you are amortizing. See the applicable Code section for limits on the amortizable amount.

Column (d). Enter the Code section under which you amortize the costs.

Column (f). Compute the amortization deduction by:

1. Dividing column (c) by the number of months over which the costs are to be amortized, and multiplying the result by the number of months in the amortization period included in your tax year beginning in 1997; or

2. Multiplying column (c) by the percentage in column (e).

Attach any other information the Code and regulations may require to make a valid election. See Pub. 535 for more information.

Paperwork Reduction Act Notice. We ask for the information on this form to carry out the Internal Revenue laws of the United States. You are required to give us the information. We need it to ensure that you are complying with these laws and to allow us to figure and collect the right amount of tax.

You are not required to provide the information requested on a form that is subject to the Paperwork Reduction Act unless the form displays a valid OMB control number. Books or records relating to a form or its instructions must be retained as long as their contents may become material in the administration of any Internal Revenue law. Generally, tax returns and return information are confidential, as required by section 6103.

The time needed to complete and file this form will vary depending on individual circumstances. The estimated average time is:

Recordkeeping	34 hr., 41 min.
Learning about the law or the form	5 hr., 4 min.
Preparing and sending the form to the IRS	5 hr., 51 min.

If you have comments concerning the accuracy of these time estimates or suggestions for making this form simpler, we would be happy to hear from you. See the instructions for the tax return with which this form is filed.

Table A—General Depreciation System

Method: 200% declining balance switching to straight line

Convention: Half-year

Year	If the recovery period is: 3 years	5 years	7 years	10 years
1	33.33%	20.00%	14.29%	10.00%
2	44.45%	32.00%	24.49%	18.00%
3	14.81%	19.20%	17.49%	14.40%
4	7.41%	11.52%	12.49%	11.52%
5		11.52%	8.93%	9.22%
6		5.76%	8.92%	7.37%
7			8.93%	6.55%
8			4.46%	6.55%
9				6.56%
10				6.55%
11				3.28%

Table B—General and Alternative Depreciation System

Method: 150% declining balance switching to straight line

Convention: Half-year

Year	If the recovery period is: 5 years	7 years	10 years	12 years	15 years	20 years
1	15.00%	10.71%	7.50%	6.25%	5.00%	3.750%
2	25.50%	19.13%	13.88%	11.72%	9.50%	7.219%
3	17.85%	15.03%	11.79%	10.25%	8.55%	6.677%
4	16.66%	12.25%	10.02%	8.97%	7.70%	6.177%
5	16.66%	12.25%	8.74%	7.85%	6.93%	5.713%
6	8.33%	12.25%	8.74%	7.33%	6.23%	5.285%
7		12.25%	8.74%	7.33%	5.90%	4.888%
8		6.13%	8.74%	7.33%	5.90%	4.522%
9			8.74%	7.33%	5.91%	4.462%
10			8.74%	7.33%	5.90%	4.461%
11			4.37%	7.32%	5.91%	4.462%
12				7.33%	5.90%	4.461%

Table C—General Depreciation System

Method: Straight line

Convention: Mid-month

Recovery period: 27.5 years

	The month in the 1st recovery year the property is placed in service:											
Year	1	2	3	4	5	6	7	8	9	10	11	12
1	3.485%	3.182%	2.879%	2.576%	2.273%	1.970%	1.667%	1.364%	1.061%	0.758%	0.455%	0.152%
2-9	3.636%	3.636%	3.636%	3.636%	3.636%	3.636%	3.636%	3.636%	3.636%	3.636%	3.636%	3.636%
10, 12	3.637%	3.637%	3.637%	3.637%	3.637%	3.637%	3.636%	3.636%	3.636%	3.636%	3.636%	3.636%
11	3.636%	3.636%	3.636%	3.636%	3.636%	3.636%	3.637%	3.637%	3.637%	3.637%	3.637%	3.637%

Table D—General Depreciation System

Method: Straight line

Convention: Mid-month

Recovery period: 31.5 years

	The month in the 1st recovery year the property is placed in service:											
Year	1	2	3	4	5	6	7	8	9	10	11	12
4-7	3.175%	3.175%	3.175%	3.175%	3.175%	3.175%	3.175%	3.175%	3.175%	3.175%	3.175%	3.175%
8	3.175%	3.174%	3.175%	3.174%	3.175%	3.174%	3.175%	3.175%	3.175%	3.175%	3.175%	3.175%
9, 11	3.174%	3.175%	3.174%	3.175%	3.174%	3.175%	3.174%	3.175%	3.174%	3.175%	3.174%	3.175%
10, 12	3.175%	3.174%	3.175%	3.174%	3.175%	3.174%	3.175%	3.174%	3.175%	3.174%	3.175%	3.174%

Table E—General Depreciation System

Method: Straight line

Convention: Mid-month

Recovery period: 39 years

	The month in the 1st recovery year the property is placed in service:											
Year	1	2	3	4	5	6	7	8	9	10	11	12
1	2.461%	2.247%	2.033%	1.819%	1.605%	1.391%	1.177%	0.963%	0.749%	0.535%	0.321%	0.107%
2-39	2.564%	2.564%	2.564%	2.564%	2.564%	2.564%	2.564%	2.564%	2.564%	2.564%	2.564%	2.564%

Depreciation Worksheet

Description of Property	Date Placed in Service	Cost or Other Basis	Business/ Investment Use %	Section 179 Deduction	Depreciation Prior Years	Basis for Depreciation	Method/ Convention	Recovery Period	Rate or Table %	Depreciation Deduction

1997

Department of the Treasury
Internal Revenue Service

Instructions for Form 8824

Like-Kind Exchanges

Section references are to the Internal Revenue Code unless otherwise noted.

General Instructions

A Change To Note

Generally, for exchanges after June 8, 1997, personal property used predominantly within the United States and personal property used predominantly outside the United States are not property of a like kind. See section 1031(h).

Purpose of Form

Use Parts I, II, and III of Form 8824 to report the exchange of business or investment property for property that is of a like kind (section 1031). Use Part IV to report the nonrecognition of gain from conflict-of-interest sales by certain members of the executive branch of the Federal Government (section 1043).

For more information on like-kind exchanges, see section 1031 and its regulations and **Pub. 544,** Sales and Other Dispositions of Assets.

When To File

For each like-kind exchange, you must file Form 8824 for the tax year you transferred property to another party in an exchange. If you made a related party (defined later) exchange, you must file Form 8824 for 2 years following the year of the exchange.

Like-Kind Exchanges

Generally, if you exchange business or investment property solely for business or investment property of a like kind, no gain or loss is recognized under section 1031. If you also receive other property or money, a gain is recognized to the extent of the other property or money received, but a loss is not recognized.

Section 1031 does not apply to exchanges of inventory, stocks, bonds, notes, other securities or evidence of indebtedness, and certain other assets. See section 1031(a)(2).

Like-kind property. Properties are like kind if they are of the same nature or character, even if they differ in grade or quality. Personal property of a like class is also considered like kind. However, livestock of different sexes is **not** like-kind property. Also, personal property used predominantly in the United States and personal property used predominantly outside the United States are **not** like-kind properties. See Pub. 544 for more details.

Real property is of the same kind as other real property, regardless of whether the properties are improved or unimproved. However, real property in the United States and real property outside the United States are **not** like-kind properties.

Deferred exchanges. A deferred exchange occurs when the property **received** in the exchange is not received immediately upon the transfer of the property **given up.** For a deferred exchange to qualify as like kind, you must:

- Identify the replacement property you receive within 45 days after the date you transferred the property given up, **and**
- Receive the new property by the earlier of **(a)** 180 days after the date you transferred the property given up, **or (b)** the due date of your tax return for the year of the transfer (including extensions).

Property is identified by notifying, in writing, another party to the exchange (other than a related party) of your selection of the property. Identification may also be made in a written agreement for the exchange of properties.

Multi-asset exchanges. A multi-asset exchange occurs when the exchanged properties consist of the transfer and receipt of more than one group of like-kind properties. For example, an exchange of land, vehicles, and cash for land and vehicles would be a multi-asset exchange. An exchange of land, vehicles, and cash for only land would not be a multi-asset exchange. A multi-asset exchange also occurs if only one group of like-kind properties is created but more than one property is transferred or received within that group.

Special rules apply when figuring the amount of gain recognized and the basis of properties received in a multi-asset exchange. For details, see Regulations section 1.1031(j)-1.

Reporting of multi-asset exchanges. If you transferred **and** received **(a)** more than one group of like-kind properties, or **(b)** cash or other (not like-kind) property, do not complete lines 12 through 18 of Form 8824. Instead, attach a sheet showing how you figured the realized and recognized gain, and enter the correct amount for lines 19 through 25. Report recognized gain on **Schedule D, Form 4797,** Sales of Business Property, or **Form 6252,** Installment Sale Income, whichever applies.

Related party exchanges. Special rules apply to like-kind exchanges made with a related party. A **related party** includes your spouse, child, grandchild, parent, brother or sister, or a related corporation, S corporation, partnership, or trust. See section 1031(f).

If either you or the related party disposes of property received in an exchange before the date that is 2 years after the last transfer of property from the exchange, the deferred gain or (loss) from line 24 must be reported on your return for the year of disposition (unless an exception on line 11 applies).

If you are filing this form for 1 of the 2 years following the year of the exchange, complete Parts I and II. If both lines 9 and 10 are "No," **stop there,** and attach the form to your return. If either line 9 or line 10 is "Yes" and an exception on line 11 applies, check the applicable box on line 11, **stop there,** and attach the form to your return. If no line 11 exceptions apply, complete Part III. The deferred gain or (loss) from line 24 must be reported on this tax year's return as if the exchange had been a sale.

An exchange structured to avoid related party rules is **not** treated as a like-kind exchange. See section 1031(f)(4).

Specific Instructions

Lines 1 and 2. For real property, show the address, type of property, and country if outside the United States. For personal property, enter a short description.

Line 5. See **Deferred exchanges** above.

Line 7. See **Related party exchanges** above.

Line 11c. If you believe that you can establish to the satisfaction of the IRS that tax avoidance was **not** a principal purpose of both the exchange and the disposition, attach an explanation. See **Pub. 537,** Installment Sales, for exceptions where tax avoidance is not a principal purpose.

Lines 12, 13, and 14. If you gave up other property in addition to the like-kind property, enter the fair market value (FMV) and the adjusted basis of the other property on lines 12 and 13, respectively.

The gain or (loss) from this property is figured on line 14 and must be reported on your return. Report gain or (loss) as if the exchange was a sale.

Line 15. Include on line 15 the **sum** of the following:

- Any cash paid to you by the other party,
- The FMV of other (not like-kind) property you received, if any, **and**
- Net liabilities assumed by the other party—the **excess,** if any, of **liabilities** assumed by the other party (including mortgages on the property you gave up); **over the total** of: **(a)** any liabilities you assumed (or that applied to the property you received), **(b)** cash you paid to the other party, and **(c)** the FMV of other property you gave up.

Reduce the sum of the above amounts (but not below zero) by any exchange expenses you incurred. See the example below the line 18 instructions.

Line 18. Include on line 18 the **sum** of the following:

- The adjusted basis of the like-kind property you gave up,
- Exchange expenses, if any (except for expenses used to reduce the amount reported on line 15), **and**
- Net amount paid to the other party—the **excess,** if any, of the **total** of: **(a)** any liabilities you assumed, **(b)** cash you paid to the other party, and **(c)** the FMV of the other property you gave up; **over** any liabilities assumed by the other party.

See Regulations section 1.1031(d)-2 and the following example for figuring amounts to enter on lines 15 and 18.

Example. A owns an apartment house with an FMV of $220,000, an adjusted basis of $100,000, and subject to a mortgage of $80,000. B owns an apartment house with an FMV of $250,000, an adjusted basis of $175,000, and subject to a mortgage of $150,000.

A transfers his apartment house to B, and receives in exchange the apartment house owned by B and $40,000 cash. Each apartment house is transferred subject to the mortgage on it.

A enters on line 15 only the $40,000 cash received from B. The $80,000 of liabilities assumed by B is not included because it does not exceed the $150,000 of liabilities A assumed. A enters $170,000 on line 18—the $100,000 adjusted basis, plus the $70,000 excess of the liabilities A assumed over the liabilities assumed by B ($150,000–$80,000).

B enters $30,000 on line 15—the excess of the $150,000 of liabilities assumed by A over the total ($120,000) of the $80,000 of liabilities B assumed and the $40,000 cash B paid. B enters on line 18 only the adjusted basis of $175,000, because the total of the $80,000 of liabilities B assumed and the $40,000 cash B paid does not exceed the $150,000 of liabilities assumed by A.

Line 21. If you disposed of section 1245, 1250, 1252, 1254, or 1255 property (see the instructions for Part III of Form 4797), you may be required to recapture as ordinary income part or all of the realized gain (line 19). Figure the amount to enter on line 21 as follows:

- For **section 1245** property, enter the **smaller** of **(a)** the total adjustments for deductions (whether for the same or other property) allowed or allowable to you or any other person for depreciation or amortization (up to the amount of the gain shown on line 19), **or (b)** any gain shown on line 20, **plus** the FMV of non-section 1245 like-kind property acquired.
- For **section 1250** property, enter the **larger** of **(a)** the **excess,** if any, of the gain you would have had to report as ordinary income because of additional depreciation (see the Form 4797 instructions for line 26) if you had sold the property **over** the FMV of the section 1250 property acquired, **or (b)** any gain shown on line 20.
- The rules for **section 1252, 1254,** and **1255** property are similar to those for section 1245 property. See Regulations section 1.1252-2(d) and Temporary Regulations section 16A.1255-2(c) for details. If the installment method applies to this exchange:

1. See section 453(f)(6) to determine this year's taxable amount of installment sale income and report it on Form 6252.

2. Enter on Form 6252, line 25 or 36, the section 1252, 1254, or 1255 recapture amount you figured on Form 8824, line 21. Do not enter more than the amount shown on Form 6252, line 24 or 35.

3. Also, enter this amount on Form 4797, line 15.

If not recapturing all the ordinary income this year, you must report on Form 6252 the ordinary income up to the taxable installment sale income in future years until it is all reported.

Line 22. Report a gain from the exchange of property used in a trade or business (and other noncapital assets) on Form 4797, line 5 or 16. Report a gain from the exchange of capital assets according to the Schedule D instructions for your return. Be sure to use the date of the exchange as the date for reporting the gain. If the installment method applies to this exchange, see section 453(f)(6) to determine this year's taxable amount and report it on Form 6252.

Line 24. If line 19 is a loss, enter it on line 24. Otherwise, subtract any line 23 amount from the line 19 amount, and enter the result. See **Related party exchanges** on page 1 for exchanges with related parties.

Line 25. The amount on line 25 is your basis of the like-kind property you received in the exchange. The basis of other property received in the exchange, if any, is its FMV.

Section 1043 Conflict-of-Interest Sales (Part IV)

If you sell property at a gain according to a certificate of divestiture issued by the Office of Government Ethics (OGE), you may elect to recognize gain on the sale only to the extent that the amount realized on the sale exceeds the cost of replacement property (permitted property) purchased within 60 days after the sale. **Permitted property** is any obligation of the United States or any diversified investment fund approved by the OGE.

Complete Part IV of Form 8824 only if the cost of the replacement property exceeds the basis of the divested property. Otherwise, report the gain on Schedule D or Form 4797, whichever applies.

Basis in the replacement property is reduced by the amount of the gain not recognized. If you made more than one purchase of replacement property, reduce the basis of the replacement property in the order it was acquired.

Line 29. Enter the amount you received from the sale of the divested property, minus any selling expenses.

Line 34. Follow these steps to determine the amount to enter.

1. Use Part III of Form 4797 as a worksheet to figure ordinary income under the recapture rules.

2. Enter on Form 8824, line 34, the amount from Form 4797, line 31. **Do not** attach the Form 4797 (worksheet) to your return.

3. Report the amount from line 34 on Form 4797, line 10, column (g). In column (a), write "From Form 8824, line 34." **Do not** complete columns (b) through (f).

Line 35. If you sold a capital asset, enter any gain from line 35 on Schedule D.

If you sold property used in a trade or business (or any other noncapital asset), report the gain on Form 4797, line 2 or 10, column (g). In column (a), write "From Form 8824, line 35." **Do not** complete columns (b) through (f).